ABE LINCOLN'S LEGACY OF LAUGHTER

ABE LINCOLN'S LEGACY OF LAUGHTER

Humorous Stories by and about Abraham Lincoln

Edited by Paul M. Zall

The University of Tennessee Press / Knoxville

Copyright © 2007 by The University of Tennessee Press / Knoxville.
All Rights Reserved. Manufactured in the United States of America.
First Edition.

This book is printed on acid-free paper.

Library of Congress Cataloging-in-Publication Data

Abe Lincoln's legacy of laughter : humorous stories by and about Abraham
Lincoln / edited by Paul M. Zall. – 1st ed.
    p. cm.
Substantially rev. ed. of: Abe Lincoln laughing. c1982.
Includes bibliographical references and indexes.

ISBN-13: 978-1-57233-585-1 (pbk.: alk. paper)
ISBN-10: 1-57233-585-8 (pbk.: alk. paper)

  1. Lincoln, Abraham, 1809–1865–Anecdotes.
  2. Lincoln, Abraham, 1809–1865–Humor.
  3. American wit and humor.
  I. Zall, Paul M.
  II. Abe Lincoln laughing.

E457.15.A135 2007
973.7092–dc22
                    2006033637

For Gina, Charles, and Natalie Rae Wilson

CONTENTS

Preface
ix

Introduction
xi

1. Lincoln's Writings and Speeches
1

2. Writings of Others before April 1865
21

3. Stories Told after April 1865 by Those
Who Knew Lincoln Well
41

4. Stories Told by Others after April 1865
87

Notes
115

Selected Bibliography
129

Index of Entries by Section
135

Subject Index
141

PREFACE

THIS BOOK CONSISTS OF STORIES BY AND ABOUT ABRAHAM LINCOLN BEFORE AND after becoming president. Most are traced to printed sources or analogues. Some he told, others were assigned to him in his day and ours by a range of reporters. The stories selected here are grouped according to my level of confidence in the reliability of resources. The groups derive from Lincoln's writings and speeches; writings by others up to April 1865; post–April 1865 writings by those who knew him; and post–April 1865 writings by others, including a sample from the twentieth century. Within each group, entries are arranged in the order they appeared in print. Headnotes on probable sources and analogues are meant to show that the premium was on familiarity, not originality, and immediacy, not posterity. To readers, his stories gave the comfort and support of an old shoe. Today they signify enduring affection and respect for the man who made freedom feasible.

This is completely different from the random selection in the first edition of *Abe Lincoln Laughing.* About 20 percent of the original 325 Lincoln entries failed to meet standards set in Don and Virginia Fehrenbacher's *Recollected Words of Abraham Lincoln* (1996). A roughly equivalent number validated by those standards have been substituted, thanks to contributions from my dear friends Virginia and Don Fehrenbacher, for whom I was proud to serve as the "man at the Huntington." Michael Burlingame, Mark L. Johnson, and Michael Vorenberg made valuable contributions. For sustenance and spiritual support, I thank the Huntington Library staff and colleagues, especially Christopher Adde, Sarkis Badalyan, Cathy Cherbosque, Juan Gomez, Lorraine Perotta, Jack Rogers, and Mary Vega. My principal resource for the past half century, the Huntington has supplied both manuscript and printed material for thirty of my books and for the present work, with the generous support of curators Mary Robertson and Alan Jutzi and librarian David Zeidberg.

INTRODUCTION

MY FIRST ACQUAINTANCE WITH LINCOLN WAS IN CHILDHOOD. MY SISTER CELIA, who raised me, prefaced every caution, curse, or cure with, "As Abraham Lincoln said. . . ." It did her a lot of good. She lived to 107. But it left me crippled with a lifelong question. If he had said everything she said he said, when did Lincoln have time for anything else? With age, the question covered an amorphous mass of Lincoln stories, such as:

> They brought home the drowned fisherman and asked the widow what to do with him. She said, "Take the eels out and set him again!"

> The wounded soldier refused to tell where he had been hit. The girl asked President Lincoln. He replied, "My dear, the ball that wounded him would not have wounded you."

> The sun never sets on the British Empire because God does not trust them in the dark.

It takes a willing suspension of disbelief to read these as told by Lincoln. Mark Twain said, "Some things do not happen at the right time, and some do not happen at all. The conscientious historian will correct this defect."[1] It has been ever thus with Lincoln stories. Lincoln himself had trouble telling how many he had told. At different times he confessed to "only about half a dozen," or "about half," or about "one-sixth."[2] The rest were fathered upon him.

Legitimate or not, hundreds of stories come down for his name's sake. *Time* magazine's Lincoln tribute for 4 July 2005 brought out a half dozen usual suspects. Every four years a losing candidate will say he felt as Lincoln had, "Too damned badly hurt to laugh—and too damned proud to cry." Or Republicans will say the Democrats are fighting among themselves, and the Democrats will reply, "As Lincoln said, 'They're like cats on the back fence. They're not fighting, they're making more cats.'" Who knows how many of these Lincoln stories are running around in print or by word-of-mouth and over the World Wide Web?

Stories like these are woven into the fabric of our culture. Yet hardly a dozen can be traced directly to Lincoln's own hand. Others come from reports of his speeches in the partisan press of both sides. In the last five years of his life, they reported an estimated ninety-five speeches and no funny stories.[3]

Vanity Fair complained, "Abe is becoming more grave. He don't construct as many jokes as he did."[4] Obviously he knew that jokes were inappropriate to the nation's chief executive, commander in chief, head of his party, and ceremonial high priest, especially in time of war. He had the precedent of George Washington, who sanitized file copies of even his private correspondence before taking office.[5] So far as we know, Lincoln did not sanitize his previous correspondence, but the pressure of his presidency allowed little leisure for the laughter that he loved.[6] Telegrapher Edward Rosewater swore you could hear him laughing at his knee-slapping stories a mile away.[7]

Much of Lincoln's appeal lay in the people's perception of "Old Abe" as a common man, homely and humble as themselves with a passion for telling old jokes that fit as comfortably as a pair of bedroom slippers. The press would not let him forget this image that he had helped to create and now risked discarding for dignity. The press would perpetuate the public's preconceived perception shaped in great measure by his physical appearance, platform performance, and passion for swapping stories with friends old and new.

Nathaniel Hawthorne described him as "about the homeliest man I ever saw." The newspapers said his gait resembled "the offspring of a happy marriage between a derrick and a windmill." Of his platform performance they described, "A shrug of his shoulder, and elevation of his eyebrows, a depression of his mouth, and a general malformation of countenance so comically awkward that it never fails to bring down the House."[8] The public delighted in his "awkward gesticulation, the contortions of countenance, and the stooping forward almost to the ground to enforce some . . . argument or . . . invective."[9]

By design or default, Lincoln lived up to the public's expectations. To some, his Kentucky accent sounded peculiar ("agin," "cheer" for chair, "unly").[10] The Democrats' newspaper, the *Chicago Times,* complained about how hard it was to report his speeches "in intelligible English."[11] But to many readers that was exactly the way he was supposed to talk. He sounded just like the westerners they knew from stories in their newspapers and magazines.[12]

This was a newspaper-reading nation. Literacy rates are said to have surpassed 80 percent. They had more newspapers per capita than we have now. Railroads and telegraph spread mass-circulating magazines coast to coast. During the Civil War, civilian newspapers crossed enemy lines freely, soldiers printed their own—126 Federal and 15 Confederate newspapers survive, including *Black Warrior,* printed by black troops from Rhode Island stationed in Louisiana.

The style seemed similar but the difference was substantial. The westerners in the press were artful, Lincoln was natural. His appeal was grounded in his "wonderful intuitive knowledge" of the people, through whose ranks from top to bottom he had risen.[13] A half century's living in the backwoods and on the prairie accounted for his solidarity with pioneering Americans—like the mother who hears a child squalling afar off and says, "Thar's one of 'em ain't dead yet."

Farmers knew what he was talking about when reminded of the scarecrow so ugly that the crows brought back corn they had stolen last year. Sophisticated city folk appreciated the cynicism and irony of his repartee, as when asked what he thought of a new book: "For those who like this sort of thing this is exactly the sort of thing they would like." With amiable personality to match his stories, he could please some of the people most of the time.

Reporter J. H. Buckingham of the *Boston Courier* rode the stage between Peoria and Springfield with the local Whig politician who entertained fellow passengers of all parties with stories all the way. In his district, "He knew, or appeared to know everybody he met, the name of the tenant of every farm-house, and the owner of every plat of ground. Such a shaking of hands, such a how-d'ye-do . . . was never seen before. He had a kind word for every body on the road, even to the horses, and the cattle, and the swine."[14]

When he abandoned humor for dignity's sake, the crowds abandoned him. Those at the Wisconsin State Fair came to hear plain Abe. When the Honorable Abraham Lincoln started lecturing about "Man," they wandered off to the cow pens and sideshows.[15] When he became president and abandoned stories, the press rushed in with all the Lincoln stories fit to print—and otherwise. They gave resurrected jests new life. An old story about Franklin feeding his horse oysters became a new story about Lincoln, with the oysters morphed into catfish.

Some stories required readjustment. Told that General Grant was drinking too much whiskey, Lincoln asked what brand Grant drank so he could serve it to his other generals. In the previous century, when King George was told that General Wolfe was mad, he said, "Have him bite my other generals." When both Douglas and Lincoln kept calling Republicans old dogs and Democrats old lions, Lincoln applied Aesop's fable about the lonely lion that courted a fair maiden. Her parents insisted on disarming him with one makeover after another until they left the lion toothless. Aesop said they merely sent the lion on its way. Lincoln said they beat his brains out.

Such transformations were not always improvements. Lincoln told about a neighbor whose foot caught in the stirrups while mounting his horse. After considerable struggle, he cried, "If you're getting on, I'm getting off." Forty years earlier, a landlocked sailor in the same predicament had said, "If you are going to get on, I'll get off, for damme if I'll ride double with you."[16]

In a symbiotic relationship, Lincoln would clip stories from the newspapers or he would quip and they would clip. Like the press, Lincoln used the same recycling process and resources for a deep reservoir of material—old comic almanacs, jest books, current newspapers, even popular songs like the Irish ballad about the cork leg that always ran away from a fight. Mere allusions were often enough to trigger raucous laughter, as when in court he summed up simply by saying, "They have their facts right but they are drawing the wrong conclusion," and won the case. The jury knew the story about the farmer's boy dashing up breathlessly, "Pa, pa, the hired man and Sis in the hayloft—she's a liftin' up her skirts and he's apullin' down his pants and fixin' to pee all over the hay!" The farmer calmed him: "Son, you got the facts right but you are drawing the wrong conclusion."

From recent magazines like *Harper's Monthly,* then spreading coast to coast, he recycled celebrated images. He described the opposition's principles as being thin "as homeopathic soup that was made by boiling the shadow of a pigeon that had starved to death."[17] Names would change but the facetiae were familiar. The late Steve Allen used to say there was no such thing as an old joke—it was new the first time you heard it. In this respect, old material had political benefits: identifying with new masses of newspaper-reading Americans, ingratiating himself with rural folk, providing immigrants with the pattern of a hero as common as themselves.

Lincoln was a most uncommon common man when common people were in perpetual motion westward. New Jersey's Jonathan Dayton counted twelve to fourteen wagonloads a day passing his door. A Virginia tavern keeper counted fifty-one and fifty-seven wagonloads.[18] They knew Lincoln spoke truly when he told about the family's chickens that would lie on their backs whenever the wagon sheets were brought out and wait to be tied and tossed on the wagon for the next move. Lincoln, however, stayed rooted in Springfield.

By the 1860 census Springfield's population had grown to 9,320—a mobile amalgam of "German, Irish, French, Scandinavians, Italians, Portuguese, Spaniards, Jews and Gentiles."[19] Two thousand registered voters were listed as "landless, unskilled and foreign born," presumably pausing on their way west, where they could buy a farm for what it cost to rent one in Springfield.[20] Lincoln himself, with long and deep roots in the town's exclusive core community of 270 elite citizens, stayed behind and became a leader in the state legislature, a city father, a congressman, a prosperous corporation lawyer, and a powerbroker in the state's Republican party.[21] Some common man!

Those who knew him well credited Lincoln's humor with easing his way in the world. In 1831 at Sangamo Town, young John Rolle had helped him build a flatboat. Rolle recalled how Lincoln's genial spirits and stories soon made him the life of the village. People would get together noon or night and "take their seat on a sleek, barkless log" to hear his stories. Many years after he had left, they were calling it "Abe's log."[22]

On a log or on the stump, at a shooting match, courthouse, or school-house, people—sometimes ten or as many as thirty—anticipated a good laugh from Lincoln. Everyone knew "he always had a good laugh ready, and if not, he could improvise one" to fit people and circumstances.[23] At a Little Falls, New York, whistle stop, he acknowledged the welcome: "I have come to see you, and allow you to see me (Applause)—regarding the ladies, I have the best bargain.(Laughter) I don't make that acknowledgement to the gentlemen" (laughter).[24]

He could always fall back on his appearance, in introducing himself and Mary Lincoln as "the long and short of it" or saying, "If I have one vice . . . it is not being able to say no! Thank God for not making me a woman. . . . But if He had I suppose he would have made me just as ugly as He did, and no one would have tempted me."[25] Introducing himself to a convention of Whig editors, he disarmed them by comparing himself to the ugly man who met a woman on horseback. This dialogue ensued: "Well, for land's sake, you are the homeliest man I ever saw." "Yes, madam, but I can't help it." "No, I suppose not, but you might stay at home."[26]

In an era when debates instigated duels, Lincoln could be just as effective with sly hints that left even the victims laughing. In the state legislature, with both serving on the new Committee on Politeness, Etiquette and Ceremony, he was engaged in hot debate with Democratic leader Wickliffe Kitchell. Arguing that Kitchell's argument was short sighted, Lincoln illustrated with the story of the hunter who repeatedly fired at what looked like a squirrel but that turned out to be a louse on his shaggy eyebrow. As all present could plainly see, Kitchell had heavy, shaggy eyebrows.

Lincoln's self-deprecating wit could be biting also, as in his celebrated defense of Whig presidential candidate General Zachary Taylor's record. On the floor of Congress Lincoln mocked the war record of Taylor's opponent General Lewis Cass ("He *in*vaded Canada without resistance, and he *out*vaded it without pursuit"). He compared it with his own record in the Black Hawk war: "In the days of the Black Hawk war, I fought, bled, and came away. . . . I did not break my sword, for I had none to break; but I bent a musket pretty badly. . . . I had a good many bloody struggles with the musquetoes; and, although I never fainted from loss of blood, I can truly say I was often very hungry."[27]

Fellow congressmen at first saw Lincoln as a comical wild and wooly westerner. They laughed as he paced the aisles, doing the motions of the old-style elocutionists in old-fashioned fustian: "I know that the great volcanoe at Washington, aroused and directed by the evil spirit that reigns there, is belching forth the lava of political corruption." They laughed at his awkward way of walking and the way he walked to the boardinghouse carrying books in a bandana handkerchief tied to the end of a pole. But by New Years they treasured him as "the champion story-teller in the Capitol."[28]

Because of the way he performed in debate and the way he looked and talked, congressional Whigs felt they had been blessed with another Davy Crockett. In the 1830s they had exploited Davy as a real common man in contrast to phony Andy Jackson. They printed biographies Davy never wrote, slogans and speeches he never spoke ("half-horse, half-alligator, with a touch of the earthquaker"), an almanac in his name, and a very popular play that entertained Crockett of Tennessee himself.

They sent Davy on tour as far as New England, but there he disappointed the public, who were expecting the coonskin-clad comic figure that Whigs had packaged. He came dressed in elegant attire better suited to Lord Byron.

A decade later the Whigs sent Lincoln on the same tour to New England with the same result. Lincoln disappointed New Englanders not because of the way he looked, which they did find amusing, but because his performances upset their programmed preconceptions. They were expecting "stories and high flavored allusions," but in ten days of speaking he treated them to very few—as the image of pseudo-Whig principles being like the peddler's pantaloons, "large enough for any man, small enough for any boy."[29] The consensus was that he argued with "sobriety to suit cultured audiences."[30]

His success in New England came not from style but substance. He had made a thorough study of the public pulse and powerbrokers of the region. Through interviewing leading political leaders he acquired a solid understanding of local issues. Bostonian Robert Rantoul Jr. said that if Lincoln had made such a study across the nation he would have matched Napoleon's genius.[31]

Adversaries knew the power of his style. The unfriendly *New York Tribune* conceded that Lincoln's good-humored temperament made him a formidable adversary—"Colloquial, affable, good-natured, almost jolly. . . . His opponents are almost persuaded he is no opponent at all."[32] Stephen A. Douglas concurred: "Every one of his stories seems like a whack upon my back . . . Nothing else—not any of his arguments or any of his replies to my questions—disturbs me. But when he begins to tell a story, I feel that I am to be overmatched."[33]

Beginning with the Lincoln-Douglas debates, shorthand reporters enabled readers across the country to virtually hear him on national affairs. The new wire services and *Harper's New Monthly* spread his speeches across the nation. Stereotyping made his book accessible and inexpensive. He had collected newspaper reports of both his and Douglas's speeches for his only book, *Political Debates . . . 1858*. It sold 30,000 copies within months of publication at fifty cents a copy.[34]

It was an age when people read aloud. They could now hear how Lincoln baited and debated Douglas, bringing the issues down to local business and bosoms. In Cincinnati he quoted Douglas, saying that he would be for the black man in a match with crocodiles. Lincoln added, "or as we old Ohio boatmen used to call them alligators." The following year at New Haven in the same context, he referred instead to the local question of raising cattle or growing tobacco.[35]

As in the 1840s on touring New England, so in the 1860s on becoming president, Lincoln elevated substance over style. When he abandoned puns for pungency, the press rushed in to fill the vacuum with Lincoln stories old or new, borrowed, and increasingly blue. Joseph Howard of the *Brooklyn Eagle* confessed to coining the story about Lincoln's neighbor who was skeptical of vaccination, telling him, "It don't do a child a bit of good. I had a child vaccinated once, and in three days it fell out a window and broke its neck."[36]

Newspapers had a bottomless stock of old and new material from friends and foe. Old friend Jesse Fell supplied a Lincoln quotation that explained why a colleague's beard was white while his hair was still black: "He uses his jaw more than his brain."[37] But Fell also circulated the sort of stories Lincoln told his cronies. He quoted Lincoln on Mary

Lincoln's visiting card with the copyright notice "Entered by Act of Congress": "That's a lie—she was never entered by Act of Congress."[38]

The president's foes exploited his indecent humor as a political and moral liability, printing such Lincoln stories as how during the Revolution the British cured constipation by hanging Ethan Allen's portrait in the privy. Hearsay raged. William Norwood in May 1861 heard that Lincoln told a group of influential Presbyterian clergy that "peace with the South is as impossible as it is for you to sleep with my wife tonight."[39] Worse was the allegation passed down from father to son that just before his crucial Cooper Union speech he had regaled young Republicans with an unprintable "Rabelaisian" story about how he first met Mary Lincoln in an outhouse.[40]

At home and abroad, the press pounced on Lincoln's "flatulent and indecent stories" as mirroring degenerate morals and the mind of "an illiterate boor."[41] Confederate newspapers used terms like "slam-whanging, indecent, ill-bred, profane, vulgar."[42] Even his friends found fault. He turned down an office-seeker with the story about a sow with more pigs than teats. A friendly Baltimore newspaper expressed shock not at Lincoln's telling such stories but "that one of his friends should have seen fit to give it to the world."[43]

In his close circle of cronies that kind of story was a medium for exchanging such reminiscences as the one about switching rooms so that the bridegroom's friend ended up in the bed of the bride. When such stories became public, Lincoln's friends blamed them on the necessity for a lawyer to keep company with "low, vulgar, and unscrupulous men." Others blamed congressmen for supplying him with the "very dirty" stories. Everyone agreed, however, that he did not tell "smutty stories" in the company of ladies.[44]

The distraction of such criticism in the turmoil of the times helped to drive Lincoln to the brink of silence. "I am talking to the country, and I have to be mighty careful."[45] It was not enough to be understood. He had to avoid being misunderstood, a congenital defect of political discourse. He contracted an aversion to writing as "furnishing new grounds for misunderstanding" and to speaking without a script.[46] The last time he had made "an off-hand speech," the phrase "turned tail and ran" outraged "some very nice Boston folk." He "resolved to make no more impromptu speeches" in public.[47]

In private, good humor prevailed. He told a woman seeking a presidential favor that she had as much chance of succeeding as of sleeping with his wife. Looking up from a wire datelined by General Pope, "from headquarters in the saddle," he said, "he's got his headquarters where his hindquarters ought to be." And there is the oft-told tale of the impatient cabinet kept waiting while he read to them from Artemus Ward's sketch "High Handed Outrage in Utica."[48] In that sketch an irate citizen shouts as he bashes Ward's wax statue of Judas: "Judas Iscarrot can't show his-self in Uticky with impunerty by a darn site!" Then Lincoln sprang the Emancipation Proclamation. If taken as preamble to the proclamation, for "Judas Iscarrot" read "slavery."

Many of those who knew Lincoln well have tried to analyze the nature and function of his irrepressible humor. His partner and biographer Billy Herndon spent half his own life psychoanalyzing Lincoln and concluded that humor was an antidote to his clinical depression. The leading biographer in our time, Benjamin Thomas, concurred that Lincoln used humor "to relieve his troubled mind" but also, more pragmatically, "to soften a refusal or rebuke . . . to ingratiate himself, to put people at ease . . . as a means of escaping from a difficult position or avoiding an embarrassing commitment," and as a bridge connecting him to common people, who, as Lincoln said, were "more easily influenced and informed through the medium of a story than in any other way."[49]

Good humor was so ingrained in Lincoln's temperament he impulsively shared laughter for its own sake. An entry in the diary of his secretary John Hay may serve as final analysis:

> A little after midnight . . . the President came into the office laughing, with a volume of [Thomas] Hood's works in his hand to show Nicolay and me the little Caricature "An unfortunate Bee-ing," seemingly utterly unconscious that he with his short shirt hanging about his long legs and setting out behind like the tail feathers of an enormous ostrich, was infinitely funnier than anything in the book he was laughing at.
>
> Occupied all day with matters of vast moment, deeply anxious about the fate of the greatest army of the world, with his own fame and future hanging on the events of the passing hour, he yet has such a wealth of simple bonhommie and good fellow ship that he gets out of bed and perambulates the house in his shirt to find us that we may share with him the fun.[50]

Among his intimate friends, John Hay was the prime supplier of Lincoln's stories to the press. Billy Herndon, prospecting for information about Lincoln's early years, unearthed dozens from interviewing old-timers. Even after those who had known Lincoln passed away, Lincoln stories flowed on.

In 1994 the tabloid *National Inquirer* ran a cover story about scientists resuscitating Lincoln. This started a chain of speculation about what he said when he woke up—for example, "Where's Anne Rutledge?" "I freed the what!?!" Such typically American irreverence fits neatly the Lincoln legacy of laughter. He told of overhearing two ladies on the train. One insisted Jeff Davis would win the war because he was a praying man. The other replied, "But Abram's a praying man." "But," said the first, "the Lord will think Abram's joking."

The voice of the people is the voice of God. When Lincoln, for the sake of dignity dammed his reservoir of stories, the people would not be denied. The press complied. Today along the World Wide Web, the stream flows unimpeded to a shoreless sea. Lecturers on evidence still use a Lincoln story to illustrate why not to ask too many questions. A defense lawyer trying to impugn the veracity of a witness persisted—"It was the middle of the night. It was dark as pitch. The woods were deep. There was no moon, etc. How could you tell that Jones bit Smith's nose off?" The witness replied, "He spit it out."[51]

CHAPTER 1

LINCOLN'S WRITINGS AND SPEECHES

1838

*1 APRIL. Lincoln's lack of the social graces troubled his friends. He was, said Martinette Hardin McKee, "so awkward I was always sorry for him. He did not seem to know what to say in the company of women. . . . He was too bashful to say the things he wanted to say." Polly Richardson Agnew added that he was so gawky the girls would laugh at him and he would "just laugh with them." Kate Robey Gentry remembered one romantic evening on the banks of the Ohio. She exclaimed, "The moon is going down." Lincoln replied, "That's not so—it don't really go down; it seems so. The earth turns from west to east and the revolution of the earth. . . ." Kate interrupted, "Abe—what a fool you are."[1]
It should have surprised none of his friends, then, that Abe Lincoln approached age thirty still unwed. But, as he explained to Elizabeth Caldwell Browning, he had spent the previous two years courting Mary Owens of Kentucky with honorable intention. Mary Owens, sister of a neighbor, was thirty, well educated, with dark curly hair, blue eyes, and fair skin. She stood five feet five inches tall and weighed about 150 pounds, contrary to Lincoln's description that Mrs. Browning found "droll and amusing."[2]*

Although I had seen her before, she did not look as my immagination had pictured her. I knew she was over-size, but she now appeared a fair match for Falstaff; I knew she was called an "old maid," and I felt no doubt of the truth of at least half of the appelation; but now, when I beheld her,

I could not for my life avoid thinking of my mother; and this, not from withered features, for her skin was too full of fat to permit its contracting into wrinkles; but from her want of teeth, weather-beaten appearance in general, and from a kind of notion that ran in my head, that *nothing* could have commenced at the size of infancy, and reached her present bulk in less than thirty-five or forty years; and, in short, I was not at all pleased with her. But what could I do? I had told her sister that I would take her for better or for worse, and I made a point of honor and conscience in all things to stick to my word, especially if others had been induced to act on it, which in this case, I doubted not they had, for I was now fairly convinced, that no other man on earth would have her. . . . After I had delayed the matter as long as I thought I could in honor do . . . I concluded I might as well bring it to a consummation without further delay; and so I mustered my resolution, and made the proposal to her direct; but, shocking to relate, she answered, No. . . . I was mortified, it seemed to me, in a hundred different ways . . . and to cap the whole, I then, for the first time, began to suspect that I was really a little in love with her. But let it all go. I'll try and out live it. Others have been made fools of by the girls; but this can never be with truth said of me. I most emphatically, in this instance, made a fool of myself. I have now come to the conclusion never again to think of marrying; and for this reason; I can never be satisfied with any-one who would be block-head enough to have me.[3]

1839

26 December. Lincoln, having asked to be included in a Springfield debate on federalizing the state bank, gave the final speech against the Democrats, who in speaking against the measure likened themselves to Achilles and said, "Democrats are vulnerable in the heel, but they are sound in the head and the heart." Lincoln seized on those words, mocking Democrats like the Collector of New York who had run off with a million dollars, and piling on allusions to such familiar favor-ites as the "The Cork Leg," an Irish ballad about a leg that would never stop running, and the stereotypical Irish trooper.

They are most distressingly affected in their heels with a species of "run-ning itch." It seems that this malady of their heels, operates on these *sound-headed* and *honest-hearted* creatures, very much like the cork-leg, in the comic song, did on its owner: which, when he had once got started on it, the more he tried to stop it, the more it would run away. At the haz-ard of wearing this point thread bare, I will relate an anecdote, which

2

seems too strikingly in point to be omitted. A weary Irish soldier, who was always boasting of his bravery, when no danger was near, but who invariably retreated without orders at the first charge of an engagement, being asked by his Captain why he did so, replied: "Captain, I have as brave a *heart* as Julius Caesar ever had; but some how or other, whenever danger approaches, my *cowardly* legs will run away with it."[4]

1841

26 FEBRUARY. The state legislature debated a bill by Democratic leader Wickliffe Kitchell funding the Illinois-Michigan Canal. Lincoln told an anecdote about "an eccentric old bachelor who lived in the Hoosier State." Although Harper's New Monthly Magazine *attributed it to Roger Barton of Mississippi telling about his friend Tom Martin, it was perfectly on point referring to Kitchell, "an old fellow, with shaggy, overhanging eyebrows."[5] Kitchell told an anecdote about using liquor to cure an alcoholic being similar to Lincoln's arguing that more debt would cure indebtedness. Lincoln replied.*

Like the gentleman from Montgomery, [the eccentric old bachelor] was very famous for seeing *big bugaboos* in every thing. He lived with an older brother, and one day he went out hunting. His brother heard him firing back of the field, and went out to see what was the matter. He found him loading and firing as fast as possible in the top of the tree. Not being able to discover any thing in the tree, he asked him what he was firing at. He replied a squirrel—and kept on firing. His brother believing there was some humbug about the matter, examined his person, and found on one of his eye lashes a *big louse* crawling about. It is so with the gentleman from Montgomery. He imagined he could see squirrels every day, when they were nothing but *lice.* [*The House was convulsed with laughter.*][6]

1842

22 FEBRUARY. Lincoln gave the Washington birthday speech at Springfield's Second Baptist Church. He advised treating an alcoholic with friendly persuading rather than preaching, promising, punishing, or prohibition. "You shall no more be able to pierce him," he said, using a down-home example, "than to penetrate the hard shell of a tortoise with a rye straw." He also adapted a familiar anecdote. In the jest book Funny Stories *(1795), it was about an Irish trooper caught stealing a shirt from a clothesline. The farmer shouted, "If you keep it, you will pay for it in this world or in the next." The trooper replied in plain English, "By the powers, if you will trust me so long, I will take another" (40). Lincoln's version added the brogue.*

There is something so ludicrous in *promises* of good, or *threats* of evil, a great way off, as to render the whole subject with which they are connected, easily turned into ridicule. "Better lay down that spade you're stealing, Paddy,—if you don't you'll pay for it at the day of judgment—" "By the powers, if ye'll credit me so long, I'll take another, jist."[7]

1848

5 JANUARY. As freshman member of the Post Office Committee, Lincoln made his maiden speech complaining that the administration in funding mail between Washington and Richmond assumed power the Constitution had delegated to Congress. As he began to tell about deliberations in committee, he was interrupted by the Speaker. Lincoln complied with a quip typical of his ensuing congressional year.

(Intimations were here informally given to Mr. L. that it was not in order to mention on the floor what had taken place in committee.) Mr. L. then observed that if he had been out of order in what he had said, he took it back, (a laugh) so far as he could. He had no desire, he could assure gentlemen, ever to be out of order—though he never could keep long in order.[8]

20 JUNE. Whigs had a majority of four, not enough to override President Polk's veto of their bill for internal improvements. Responding, Lincoln said Polk's arguments were like the hero's gun in the popular comic epic by John Trumbull, M'Fingal (1782), bearing wide, missing the mark, and kicking the owner over. He added that Polk's pay-as-you-go plan to fund the improvements was like a popular Irish bull.

How make a road, a canal, or clear a greatly obstructed river? The idea that we could, involves the same absurdity of the Irish bull about the new boots—"I shall nivir git 'em on," says Patrick, "till I wear 'em a day or two, and stretch 'em a little."[9]

2 JULY. Tiring of Washington life, Mary Lincoln had taken the boys, Robert and Eddie, to stay with her folks in Kentucky. In writing to her,

Lincoln gossiped about the two women she had noticed "never being seen in close companies with other ladies." With a little innuendo, he told her one of them now had a congressman in tow.

He went home with her; and if I were to guess, I would say, he went away a somewhat altered man—most likely in his pockets, and in some other particular—The fellow looked conscious of guilt, although I believe he was unconscious that every body around knew who it was that had caught him—[10]

27 JULY. The House, with its new flowing red drapes and innovative gas lamps, set the scene for the presidential race between generals Zachary Taylor and Lewis Cass. Democrats accused Whigs of riding the coattails of old warhorse Taylor. Lincoln countercharged that Democrats had Cass riding the coattails of the late warhorse Andy Jackson. Lincoln said he would not have used the figures of coattails or "tails of any sort" if Democrats had not made them their weapon of choice. He accepted the challenge. "The use of degrading figures is a game at which they may not find themselves able to take all the winnings." He then fired a volley of ridiculous images, even of himself, to transform Cass from warhorse to jackass.

Like a horde of hungry ticks, you have stuck to the tail of the Hermitage lion [Jackson] to the end of his life, and you are still sticking to it, and drawing a loathsome sustenance from it after he is dead. A fellow once advertised that he had made a discovery, by which he could make a new man out of an old one, and have enough of the stuff left to make a little yellow dog. Just such a discovery has General Jackson's popularity been to you. You not only twice made President of him out of it, but you have enough of the stuff left to make Presidents of several comparatively small men [Democrats Van Buren and Polk were short] since; and it is your chief reliance now to make still another. . . . [Cass] invaded Canada without resistance, and he outvaded it without pursuit. . . . He was volunteer aid to General Harrison on the day of the battle of the Thames; and, as you said in 1840, Harrison was picking whortleberries two miles off, while the battle was fought, I suppose it is a just conclusion, with you, to say Cass was aiding Harrison in picking whortleberries. . . .

By the way, Mr. Speaker, did you know I am a military hero? Yes, sir, in the days of the Black Hawk war, I fought, bled, and came away. Speaking of General Cass's career, reminds me of my own. I was not at Stallman's defeat, but I was about as near it as Cass was to Hull's surrender; and, like him, I saw the place very soon afterwards. It is quite certain I did not break my sword, for I had none to break; but I bent a musket pretty badly on one occasion. If Cass broke his sword, the idea is, he broke it in desperation; I bent mine by accident. If General Cass went in advance of me in picking whortleberries, I guess I surpassed him in charges upon the wild onions. If he saw any live fighting Indians, it is more than I did, but I had a good many bloody struggles with the mosquitoes; and although I never fainted from loss of blood, I can truly say I was often very hungry. . . . At eating [Cass's] capacities are shown to be quite as wonderful. From October, 1821, to May, 1822, he ate ten rations a day in Michigan, ten rations a day here in Washington, and near five dollars' worth a day besides, partly on the road between the two places. . . . We have all heard of the animal standing in doubt between two stacks of hay, and starving to death; the like of that would never happen to General Cass. Place the sticks a thousand miles apart, he would stand stock-still midway between them, and eat them both at once; and the green grass along the line would be apt to suffer some too, at the same time. By all means, make him President, gentlemen. He will feed you bounteously—if—if there is any left after he shall have helped himself.

> *After cascading caricatures of their candidate, Lincoln concludes with*
> *a glancing blow at disarray among Democrats.*

I have heard some things from New York; and if they are true, we might well say of your party there, as a drunken fellow once said when he heard the reading of an indictment for hog-stealing. The clerk read on till he got to and through the words "did steal, take, and carry away, ten boars, ten sows, ten shoats, and ten pigs," at which he exclaimed—"Well, by golly, that is the most equally divided gang of hogs I ever did hear of." If there is any gang of hogs more equally divided than the Democrats of New York are about this time, I have not heard of it.[11]

> *12 SEPTEMBER. After Congress adjourned, Lincoln campaigned for*
> *Zachary Taylor in Washington and Maryland until mid-September,*
> *when he entrained for Worcester, Massachusetts. His plan was to sit*
> *in on the Whigs' state convention as an observer. On the eve of the*
> *convention a scheduled speaker failed to appear at the pep rally. They*
> *asked Lincoln to substitute. His motivational talk on a moment's*
> *notice illustrated the campaign's motto, "Rough and Ready," lasting an*
> *hour and a half and its substance the same as he had been delivering*
> *in Washington and Maryland. New England reporters anticipating a*
> *Davy Crockett replica were disappointed but nonetheless amused by*
> *such Lincoln similes as his aside on the newly formed splinter party of*

Free Soilers, whose only principle, he said, was to oppose extension of slavery into new territories.

—If their platform held any other, it was in such a general way that it was like the pair of pantaloons the Yankee peddler offered for sale, "Large enough for any man, small enough for any boy."[12]

1849

5 JANUARY. Congressman Lincoln wrote to Philadelphian autograph-collector C. Schaller with self-deprecating wit.

Your note, requesting my "signature with a sentiment" was received, and should have been answered long since, but that it was mislaid. I am not a very sentimental man; and the best sentiment I can think of is, that if you collect the signatures of all persons who are no less distinguished than I, you will have a very undistinguishing mass of names.[13]

1852

26 AUGUST. Once again Lincoln stepped in for an absent scheduled speaker to campaign for Winfield Scott against Franklin Pierce, whose chief spokesman was Stephen A. Douglas. Speaking to Springfield Whigs, he ridiculed Douglas for daring to compare Mexican War records of heroic Scott and dandy Pierce. Lincoln went on to mock the Democrats' own press releases. One had told how Pierce's father taught him to spell the word "but," and in the newspaper—published just three days before Lincoln spoke—James Shields mentioned that Pierce had fallen off his horse into a swamp.[14] Lincoln further deflated Pierce's heroics by identifying them with bizarre militia drills enjoyed twenty years earlier and identifying him with Don Quixote and—by inference—associating rotund Stephen Douglas with Sancho Panza.[15]

Forthwith appears a biographical sketch of [Pierce] in which he is represented, at the age of seventeen, to have spelled "but" for his father, who was unable to spell it for himself. . . . But the biography also represents him as cutting at cannon balls with his sword in the battles of Mexico, and calling out, "Boys there's a game of ball for you". . . . This ludicrous scene [of falling off his horse] had not been told of before; and the telling of it by Gen. Shields looks very much like a pertinacious purpose to "pile up" the ridiculous. This explains the new plan or system of tactics adopted by the democracy [Democrats]. It is to ridicule and burlesque the whole military character out of credit. . . . Being philosophical and literary men, they have read, and remembered, how the institution of chivalry was ridiculed out of existence by its fictitious votary Don Quixote. They also remember how our own "militia trainings" have been "laughed to death" by fantastic parades and caricatures upon them. We remember one of these parades ourselves here, at the head of which, on horse-back, figured our old friend Gordon Abrams, with a pine wood sword, about nine feet long, and a paste-board cocked hat, from front to rear about the length of an ox yoke, and very much the shape of one turned bottom upwards; and with spurs having rowels as large as the bottom of a tea-cup, and shanks a foot and a half long. That was the last militia muster here. Among the rules and regulations, no man is to wear more than five pounds of cod-fish for epaulets, or more than thirty yards of bologna sausages for a sash; and no two men are to dress alike, and if any two should dress alike the one that dresses most alike is to be fined (I forget how much). Flags they had too, with devices and mottoes, one of which latter is, "We'll fight till we run, and we'll run till we die."

Now in the language of Judge Douglas, "I submit to you gentlemen," whether there is not great cause to fear that on some occasion when Gen. Scott suspects no danger, suddenly Gen. Pierce will be discovered charging upon him, holding a huge roll of candy in one hand for a spy-glass; with B U T labelled on some appropriate part of his person; with Abrams' long pine sword cutting in the air at imaginary cannon balls, and calling out "Boys there's a game of ball for you," and over all streaming the flag, with the motto, "We'll fight till we faint, and I'll treat when it's over." . . . I much doubt if we do not perceive a slight abatement in Judge Douglas' confidence in Providence, as well as in the people. I suspect that confidence is not more firmly fixed with the Judge than it was with the old woman whose horse ran away with her in a buggy. She said she trusted in Providence till the britchen broke; and then she didn't know what on airth to do.[16]

1854

11 SEPTEMBER. Lincoln wrote an editorial for the Illinois Journal *decrying repeal of the Missouri Compromise, using the Democratic candidate for Congress as a whipping boy. That candidate was his old friend and benefactor, John Calhoun, who had given Lincoln, though inexperienced, his first job as surveyor. Considered more formidable than Douglas, Calhoun had debated Lincoln in the previous presidential campaign with each sometimes talking four hours. He would lose the fall election but would soon be named surveyor general of Nebraska, determined to make it a slave state, as Lincoln's humorous allegory foretold.[17]*

The Kansas and Nebraska territories are now as open to slavery as Mississippi or Arkansas were when they were territories. To illustrate the case—Abraham Lincoln has a fine meadow, containing beautiful springs of water, and well fenced, which John Calhoun had agreed with Abraham (originally owning the land in common) should be his, and the argument had been consummated in the most solemn manner, regarded by both as sacred. John Calhoun, however, in the course of time, had become owner of an extensive herd of cattle—the prairie grass had become dried up and there was no convenient water to be had. John Calhoun then looks with a longing eye on Lincoln's meadow, and goes to it and throws down the fences, and exposes it to the ravages of his starving and famishing cattle.

"You rascal," says Lincoln, "what have you done? what do you do this for?"

"Oh," replies Calhoun, "everything is right. I have taken down your fence; but nothing more. It is my true intent and meaning not to drive my cattle into your meadow, nor to exclude them therefrom, but to leave them perfectly free to form their own notions of the feed, and to direct their movements in their own way!"

Now would not the man who committed this outrage be deemed both a knave and a fool—a knave in removing the restrictive fence, which he had solemnly pledged himself to sustain—and a fool in supposing that there could be one man found in the country to believe that he had not pulled down the fence for the purpose of opening the meadow for his cattle?[18]

16 OCTOBER. At forty-five, relentless in pursuing Douglas, Lincoln spoke at least ten times in support of Richard Yates's campaign for Douglas's seat in the Senate. The night before Lincoln spoke at Peoria, Douglas confessed, "I regard him as the most difficult and dangerous opponent that I have ever met."[19] Lincoln wrote out his Peoria speech, declaring the political agenda he would follow for the next half dozen years and omitting jokes, stories, and insults, except for referring to Douglas's arguments as "lullabys" and concluding with the image of stuffing Douglas's mouth with an infant's pacifier.

If a man will stand up and assert, and repeat, and reassert, that two and two do not make four, I know nothing in the power of argument that can stop him. I think I can answer the Judge so long as he sticks to the premises; but when he flies from them, I can not work an argument into the consistency of a maternal gag, and actually close his mouth with it.[20]

1856

13 FEBRUARY. As attorney for the Alton and Chicago Railroad, Lincoln was entitled to ask Richard P. Morgan, superintendent of the railroad, to replace an expired pass—called a "chalked hat," from the practice of thus indicating the bearers' privilege. Morgan, with whom Lincoln had roomed when riding the circuit, must have known the old joke was usually about an ax, but a transport vehicle made a better fit.

Says Tom to John "Here's your old rotten wheel-barrow . . . I've broke it, usin on it . . . I wish you would mend it, case I shall want to borrow it this arter-noon." Acting on this as a precedent, I say "Here's your old 'chalked hat' . . . I wish you would take it, and send me a new one, case I shall want to use it the first of March."[21]

22 FEBRUARY. Illinois editors meeting at Decatur formed a coalition that would become the Republican party. When Lincoln, the after-dinner speaker at the closing banquet, was introduced as their next candidate for the United States Senate, he responded "in his happiest vein," said the Decatur State Chronicle. *Benjamin Shaw, editor of the* Dixon Telegraph, *concurred.*

Mr. Lincoln arose and said the latter part of that sentiment I am in favor of. (Laughter) Mr. L. said, that he was very much in the position of the man who was attacked by a robber, demanding his money, when he answered, "My dear fellow, I have no money, but if you will go with me to the light, I will give you my note;" and, resumed Mr. L., if you will let me off, I will give you my note. (Laughter, and loud cries of go on.)[22]

He felt like the ugly man riding through a wood who met a woman, also on horseback, who stopped and said:
"Well, for land's sake, you are the homeliest man I ever saw."
"Yes, madam, but I can't help it," he replied.
"No, I suppose not," she observed, "but you might stay at home."[23]

10 DECEMBER. Speaking after a sumptuous banquet for three hundred Republicans in Chicago's Tremont House, Lincoln gave a virtuoso performance, a double-barreled attack on Democrats. He used an anecdote in dialect to mock their prediction that William Bissell could never be elected governor. He next fused a homely illustration with an erudite pun to mock President Buchanan.

Their conduct reminded him of the darky who, when a bear had put its head into the hole and shut out the daylight, cried out, "What was darkening the hole?" "Ah," cried the other darky, who was on to the tail of the animal, "if de tail breaks you'll find out."

The President thinks the great body of us . . . being ardently attached to liberty, in the abstract, were duped by a few wicked and designing men. There is a slight difference of opinion on this. We think he, being ardently attached to the hope of a second term, in the concrete, was duped by men who had liberty every way. He is in the cat's paw. By much dragging of chestnuts from the fire for others to eat, his claws are burnt off to the gristle, and he is thrown aside as unfit for further use. As the fool said to King Lear, when his daughters had turned him out of doors [1.4.200], "He's a shelled pea's cod."[24]

1858

21 AUGUST–15 OCTOBER. The Lincoln-Douglas Debates. Challenging Douglas for his Senate seat, Lincoln stalked him across Illinois until he negotiated a series of debates. They faced off before voters in each of the state's congressional districts outside of Chicago and Springfield. Although U.S. senators were elected by state legislators, Lincoln and Douglas were appealing to the voters who elected the legislators. Many of these folks had heard the respective messages before. They came now for the political circus—the bands, parades, carnivals, fun, feuding, and fighting. They came by foot, on horses, boats, farm wagons, excursion trains. Transforming sleepy villages into crowded campgrounds, they came by the thousands—twelve thousand clustered under Ottawa's hot sun; sixteen thousand in the cold, dripping rain at Freeport; fifteen thousand at Jonesboro; six thousand at Decatur; and eight thousand at Bloomington. In smaller towns like Macombe, four thousand slipped and slid through the mud from heavy rains. At Quincy a "continuous mud hole" proved no obstacle, and at Galesburg the bone-chilling wind sometimes drowned out the marathon speakers. Crowds stayed to the end. Lincoln thought they gave him the advantage. "I know this class of people better. . . . I was raised among this range of people." He could therefore tune his argument to their business and bosoms and identify with them through familiar allusions, jokes, and stories. "I am part of this people."[25] Douglas told reporter Robert Hitt, "Nothing else—not any of his arguments or any of his replies to my questions—disturbs me. But when he begins to tell a story, I feel that I am to be overmatched."[26] At the same time, he knew that newspapers would convey his ideas to readers North and South,[27] and so after the speeches, Lincoln took care in preparing them for the press. In print they lacked the improvisations, the give-and-take with the other speaker and the audience that gave Lincoln additional advantage. Douglas's oratory burnished by Washington marble proved no match for Lincoln's slash-and-burn wit honed on the stump. As the series wound down at Quincy in October, a weary Douglas complained, "I regret that Mr. Lincoln should have deemed it proper for him to again indulge in gross personalities and base insinuations."[28] In the state legislature dominated by Democrats, Douglas won the election. Lincoln won the popular vote aided by such wit as:

21 AUGUST. Anything that argues me into his idea of perfect social and political equality with the negro, is but a specious and fantastic arrangement of words, by which a man can prove a chestnut horse to be a horse chestnut. [63][29]

As the judge had complimented me as highly as he had, I must confess to my weakness—I was a little taken with it, it coming from a great man—I do not speak that in mockery [Douglas was five four]—I was a little taken with it; I was not much accustomed to flattery. I was very much like the hoosier with the gingerbread—he said that he loved it better and got less of it than any other man. [67]

27 AUGUST. Although he had taken extracts from the newspaper to show that there was a "fatal blow" being struck, it all went to pot as soon as [Robert] Toombs got up and told the Judge it was not so. [*Laughter*] He reminds me in that of John Phoenix's railroad survey [in San Francisco] that he published.[30] John Phoenix says he started out with various modes of measuring when they were making the measurement from the plaza to the Mission San Dolores. One was an invention of chain and pins, another was a go-it-ometer. . . . At night he said he turned to the chain man to see what distance they had come, and he said that he found that the chain man had just drawn the chain along and stuck no pins. So he turned to the man with the go-it-ometer to see the number of paces marked, and

found that it indicated four and a half miles, which he knew must be nine or ten times as far as they had come. About that time, he being much perplexed, a drayman came by and he asked him how far it was, and the drayman said it was exactly half a mile, and he wrote that down in his book, just as Douglas did what Toombs said . . . satisfied as easily as the railroad surveyor was by the drayman's statement. [131–32]

7 OCTOBER. [Referring to a document forged by Thomas Harris in his race for Congress:] The fraud having been apparently successful upon that occasion, both Harris and Douglas have more than once been attempting to put it to new uses, as the woman said when her husband's body was brought home [with the pockets] full of eels, and she was asked what should be done with him, she said take the eels out and set him again; [*great laughter*] and so Harris and Douglas have shown a disposition to take the eels out of that stale fraud by which they got the first election, and set that fraud again more than once. [260]

13 OCTOBER. To still keep up that humbug about popular sovereignty he has at last invented this sort of do-nothing sovereignty of the people excluding slavery by doing nothing at all. I ask you is this not running down his popular sovereignty doctrine to death, till it has got as thin as the homeopathic soup that was made by boiling the shadow of a pigeon that was starved to death? [316]

15 OCTOBER. This is the seventh time that Judge Douglas and I have met in these joint discussions, and the Judge, upon that subject [popular sovereignty] has been gradually improving. . . . The Judge was a little more severe upon the Administration than I have heard him to be on any former occasion, and I complimented him for it . . . and I told him to give it to them with all the power he had; and, as some of them were sitting there present, I told them I would be much obliged to them if they would give it to *him* in about the same way; and I felt that as he has vastly improved upon the attack that he made then, that he has really taken my advice upon the subject, all I can say now is . . . "go it husband and go it bear." [340][31]

1859

11 FEBRUARY. Elected an honorary member of Phi Alpha Society at Illinois College, Jacksonville, Lincoln lectured them on inventions and discoveries. To stress the need for working together, he invented a little jest.

The very first invention was a joint operation, Eve having shared with Adam in the getting up of the apron. And, indeed, judging from the fact that sewing has come down to our times as "woman's work," it is very probable she took the leading part; he, perhaps, doing no more than to stand by and thread the needle. That proceeding may be reckoned as the mother of all "Sewing societies"; and the first and most perfect "world's fair" all inventions and all inventors then in the world, being on the spot.[32]

6 APRIL. When Boston Republicans who were rabid Free Soilers sent a form letter inviting him to their celebration of Thomas Jefferson, Lincoln declined. He seized the chance to define differences between Republicans and Democrats in a letter, confident they would reprint it in the partisan press, as they did in the Boston Daily Advertiser *14 April. In the subsequent mayoral election, F. W. Lincoln Jr. lost reelection to another Democrat and turned Republican, as if reprising Lincoln's cross-dressing anecdote.*

I remember once being much amused at seeing two partially intoxicated men engage in a fight with their great-coats on, which fight, after a long, and rather harmless contest, ended in each having fought himself out of his own coat, and into that of the other. If the two leading parties of this day are really identical with the two in the days of Jefferson and Adams, they have performed about the same feat as the two drunken men.[33]

1860

27 FEBRUARY. Invited to lecture at New York's prestigious Pilgrim Church on a nonpolitical topic, Lincoln arrived to learn that unbeknownst to him the lecture series had concluded. Local Republicans invited him to speak instead at Cooper Union on the coming presidential election—with only a day to prepare the speech that gained fame at home and abroad. Besides the general public, admitted at twenty-five cents, the audience included Republican leaders, the eastern press, and especially foreign correspondents. Humor would have been as inappropriate here as in announcing his agenda in the earlier Peoria speech, but Lincoln's wit would not be denied, as in this variant of Artemus Ward's sketch about the boy who, having killed his parents, claimed mercy as an orphan.[34]

You will not abide the election of a Republican President! In the supposed event, you say, you will destroy the Union; and then, you say, the great

crime of having destroyed it will be upon us! That is cool. A highway-
man holds a pistol to my ear, and mutters through his teeth, "Stand and
deliver, or I shall kill you, and then you will be a murderer!"[35]

*5 MARCH. During an exhausting fortnight following his talk at Coo-
per Union, Lincoln spoke on the same theme across New England. He
urged Republicans to keep faith in right as might against Democratic
assaults. At Hartford city hall he attacked with stump-speaking sarcasm and ludicrous dialect ("I cannot dawt thot this strike is th'result of
the onforchunit wahfar brought aboat by this sucktional controvussy!"),
to which he added down-home analogies ("Shall we be acting right to
take this snake and carry it to a bed where there are children?"), and
such stories as he told at Hartford.*

It reminded him of the man who had a bony, spavined horse with swelled
legs. He was asked what he was going to do with such a miserable beast—
the poor creature would die. "Do?" said he. "I'm going to fat him up; *don't
you see that I have got him seal fat as high as the knees?*" (Roars of laughter.) Well, they've got the Union dissolved up to the ankle, no farther![36]

1861

*FEBRUARY. By rail, it took twelve days for Lincoln to reach Washington
for his inauguration. Besides scheduled speeches, he spoke frequently
to folks at the whistle stops, sometimes with comical results—intended
or otherwise. News reports tracked his progress.*

11 FEBRUARY, THORNTOWN, INDIANA. At Thorntown he was betrayed into an
anecdote to illustrate a point, and the train started before he got to the
place where the laugh came in, and the people were left to wonder what
the meaning might be. He was apologizing for not making a speech. He
had heard of a man who was a candidate for a county office; who owned a
horse that he set great store by, but he was a slow animal and sure footed.
He had canvassed extensively with a good chance for the nomination.
On the morning of the day of the convention, he mounted his favorite to
go to the county seat, but in spite of whip and spur, his horse lagged on
the road, biting at every bush, and when he arrived late in the evening,
the convention was over and he was defeated. So of him, if he stopped
at every station to make a stump speech he would not arrive at Washington until the inauguration was over. The Thorntown folks only heard
the first part of the story, where the candidate was urging his steed to

pass the juicy bushes. He laughed over the cutting short of his yarn, and when the train arrived at Lebanon he was jocularly told that some of the Thorntown folks had followed the train on foot, and were panting outside to hear the conclusion of the story. He told it over good-humoredly to the crowd at Lebanon. [192–93][37]

14 FEBRUARY, NEWARK, OHIO. I understand that arrangements were made for something of a speech from me here, when the train moved down, but it has gone so far that it has deprived me of addressing the many fair ladies assembled, while it has deprived them of observing my very interesting countenance. [206]

14 FEBRUARY, PITTSBURGH, PENNSYLVANIA. You know that it has not been my custom, since I started on the route to Washington, to make long speeches; I am rather inclined to silence, and whether that be wise or not, it is at least more unusual now-a-days to find a man who can hold his tongue than to find one who cannot. [209]

18 FEBRUARY, LITTLE FALLS, NEW YORK. I have come to see you and allow you to see me and in this so far regards the Ladies, I have the best of the bargain on my side. I don't make that acknowledgement to the gentlemen (Increased laughter) and now I believe I have really made my speech and am ready to bid farewell when the cars move on. [223]

22 FEBRUARY, LEAMAN PLACE, PENNSYLVANIA. Loud calls being made for Mrs. Lincoln, Mr. L. brought her out, and said he had concluded to give them "the long and the short of it!" This remark—with the disparity between the length of himself and wife—produced a loud burst of laughter, followed by enthusiastic cheers as the train moved off. [242]

1862

17 OCTOBER. A little mirth seeped through even in the president's official correspondence, as in a letter to the head of the Washington armory, George D. Ramsay.

The lady—bearer of this—says she has two sons who want to work. Set them at it, if possible. Wanting to work is so rare a merit, that it should be encouraged.[38]

24 OCTOBER. Presidential wires could also crackle with barbed sarcasm, as in replying to a request from General George B. McClellan. Inactive for the past five weeks with 7,918 fresh horses, McClellan yet asked for more.

I have just read your despatch about sore tongued and fatiegued horses. Will you pardon me for asking what the horses of your army have done since the battle of Antietam that fatigue anything?[39]

20 NOVEMBER. Chiding friendly Kentuckian slave owner George Robertson, the president quoted from a best-seller's description of Patrick Henry's comical courtroom performances (e.g., the accused had nothing to do with a stolen turkey "until it was roasted"). In the case at hand, as soon as the war was over Loyalist John Hook sued the army for requisitioning two of his cattle during the war. Patrick Henry summed up for the defense: "But hark! what notes of discord are these which disturb the general joy, and silence the acclamations of victory—they are the notes of John Hook, hoarsely bawling through the American camp, 'beef! beef! beef!'"[40]

I believe you are acquainted with the American Classics, (if there be such) and probably remember a speech of Patrick Henry, in which he represented a certain character in the revolutionary times, as totally disregarding all questions of country, and "hoarsely bawling, beef! beef!! beef!!!" Do you not know that I may as well surrender this contest, directly, as to make any order, the obvious purpose of which would be to return fugitive slaves?[41]

1863

12 JUNE. Responding to an Albany, New York, meeting protesting his suspending habeas corpus and making military arrests of civilians, the president justified these actions as fulfilling the oath to preserve and protect the Constitution while sustaining a healthy body politic.

A jury too frequently has at least one member more ready to hang the panel than to hang the traitor. . . . I can no more be persuaded that the Government can constitutionally take no strong measures in time of rebellion, because it can be shown that the same could not be lawfully taken in time of peace, than I can be persuaded that a particular drug is not good medicine for a sick man, because it can be shown not to be good food for a well one. Nor am I able to appreciate the danger [that temporary powers would become permanent] any more than I am able to believe that a man could contract so strong an appetite for emetics during temporary illness as to persist in feeding upon them during the remainder of his healthful life.[42]

26 OCTOBER. The president remitted the court-martial of Captain James Cutts, brother of Mrs. Stephen A. Douglas, found guilty of quarreling with another officer and peeping through a keyhole at another officer's wife undressing. In a private letter, Lincoln amended the platitude of Shakespeare's Polonius (Hamlet 1.3.65–67) to reprimand Cutts for quarreling. A few months earlier he had commented on the case with a double pun on the lesser offense and on the name of the Swedish ambassador, Count Piper, pronounced "peeper," joking that the culprit ought to be "elevated to the peerage . . . with the title of Count Peeper."[43]

You were convicted of two offences. One of them, not of great enormity, and yet greatly to be avoided, I feel sure you are in no danger of repeating. The other you are not so well assured against. The advice of a father to his son, "Beware of entrance to a quarrel, but being in, bear it that the opposed may beware of thee," is good, and yet not the best. . . . Quarrel not at all. . . . Yield larger things to which you can show no more than equal right; and yield lesser ones, though clearly your own. Better give your path to a dog, than be bitten by him in contesting for the right. Even killing the dog would not cure the bite.[44]

11 NOVEMBER. Lincoln's humor vented impatience at the military establishment's policies. His plan to shape freed slaves into combat units stalled from lack of white officers to train and lead them when little more than half out of a thousand candidates could not get past army examiners.[45] Directing the secretary at war to waive an exam for Dr. Jacob Freese proved futile. Official records show that Dr. Freese served only on a local draft board.[46]

I personally wish Jacob R. Freese, of New-Jersey, to be appointed a Colonel for a colored regiment—and this regardless of whether he can tell the exact shade of Julius Caesar's hair.[47]

1864

18 APRIL. The president addressed the people of Baltimore on their adopting a new constitution that outlawed slavery. With a satiric fable he reminded them that this was the third anniversary of the day they had attacked Federal troops from Massachusetts dashing to defend Washington from rebel attack.[48]

We all declare for liberty; but in using the same word we do not all mean the same *thing*. . . . The shepherd drives the wolf from the sheep's throat, for which the sheep thanks the shepherd as a *liberator,* while the wolf denounces him for the same act as the destroyer of liberty, especially as the sheep was a black one. Plainly the sheep and the wolf are not agreed upon a definition of the word liberty; and precisely the same difference prevails to-day among us human creatures, even in the North, and all professing to love liberty. . . . Recently, as it seems, the people of Maryland have been doing something to define liberty; and thanks to them that, in what they have done, the wolf's dictionary has been repudiated.[49]

9 JUNE. Notified that the National Union League had nominated him for reelection, Lincoln replied in typically self-effacing fashion behind the wit and wisdom of common folk.

I have not permitted myself, gentlemen, to conclude that I am the best man in the country; but I am reminded, in this connection, of the story of an old Dutch farmer, who remarked to a companion once that "it was not best to swap horses when crossing streams."[50]

CHAPTER 2

WRITINGS OF OTHERS BEFORE APRIL 1865

1849

30 MARCH. Pennsylvanian Moses Hampton, an ardent Whig crony in Congress seeking Lincoln's support, reminded him of the sort of stories with which Lincoln regaled their colleagues. Forty-five-year-old Hampton, an elder of the Presbyterian church, should have deplored such smutty stories.[1]

Do you remember the story of the old Virginian stropping his razor on a certain member of a young negro's body which you told. . . . I want this application to be like your story of the old woman's fish—get larger, the more it is handled.[2]

1859

16 SEPTEMBER. As result of the debates with Douglas, Republicans sought Lincoln to speak, as in Cincinnati, Ohio, where the Democratic Enquirer welcomed him with an anecdote about him that would become an American classic.

After fiercely contesting the election with Douglas, and affecting confidence that he would have a Legislature favorable to his election over his formidable competitor, that body met, and the result was considerably against him. A gentleman, when the election was announced, queried with Lincoln how he felt? Said Abe: "Well, I feel just like the boy who stubbed his toe—*too d——d badly hurt to laugh, and too d——d proud to cry!*"[3]

1860

28 April. Lincoln had spent the first week of December 1859 in Kansas stumping for Governor Charles Robinson's reelection (lost) and defining Republican vs. Democratic stands on popular sovereignty and slavery, as he would three months later at Cooper Union.[4] Except for mere notices, the national press ignored the tour until Democratic-leaning Harper's Weekly *(circulation ninety thousand) featured Lincoln's style rather than substance in the column "Humors of the Day."*

Lincoln, of Illinois, is famous for his quick wit and good jokes. The following struck us as rather amusing. The other day, when he was up not far from Kansas, with a friend or two, they saw a small stream, and inquired its name. One of the passengers said, "It is called 'The Weeping Water.'" Lincoln's eyes twinkled. "You remember," said he, "the laughing water up in Minnesota, called Minnehaha. Now, I think, this should be Minneboohoo."[5]

Spring–Summer. As a presidential candidate, Lincoln intended to make no public statements speaking or writing but cooperated in a campaign biography authored by William Dean Howells. Howells's assistant, young James Quay Howard, interviewed the candidate in Springfield. In the interviews, Lincoln clarified complex issues for the young reporter with old stories.

My speeches in favor of a Protective Tariff would please Pennsylvania and offend W.C. Bryant [of New York] in the same degree. It is like the case of three men who had nothing to cover them but a blanket only sufficient to cover two. When No. 1 pulled it *on* himself, he pulled it *off* No. 3.[6]

1861

March. Lincoln had turned down a seat in the legislature in order to run for the Senate. His friends expected another Republican would replace him, but a Democrat won the seat. "The Editor's Drawer" of Harper's New Monthly Magazine *said that Lincoln consoled them with a story. Salmon P. Chase's diary reported Lincoln told the story in a January 1863 cabinet meeting.[7]*

He said, the result [of the election] reminded him of one of the camp-followers of General Taylor's army, who had secured a barrel of cider, erected a tent, and commenced dealing it out to the thirsty soldiers at twenty-five cents a drink; but he had sold but little before another sharp one set up another tent at his back, and tapped the barrel so as to flow on his side, and peddled out No. 1 cider *at five cents a drink!* of course getting the latter's trade entire on borrowed capital.[8]

27 APRIL. The New York Times *reported how Lincoln handled the threat of invasion from Maryland and Virginia a week after calling for loyal states to supply seventy-five thousand troops.*

A deputation of 16 Virginians and 8 Marylanders visited the President on April [22] and demanded cessation of hostilities until after the session of Congress! Mr. Lincoln, of course, declined the proposition. One of the deputation said that 75,000 Marylanders would contest the passage of troops over her soil; to which the President replied, that he presumed there was room enough on her soil to bury 75,000 men.[9]

6 MAY. When his secretary John Hay told him that John Johnson, a state senator from Paducah, Kentucky, had protested the occupation of Cairo, Illinois, Lincoln's reply sizzled with subtle satire. Reprinting it in his diary, Hay commented, "It will take the quiet satire of the note about a half an hour to get through the thick skull of this Kentucky Senator, and then he will think it a damned poor joke."

The President directs me to say that the views so ably stated by you shall have due consideration: and to assure you that he would certainly never have ordered the movement of troops, complained of, had he known that Cairo was in your Senatorial district.[10]

5 JULY. A yarn by old family friend Samuel Haycraft told a folklore "ugly man" story attached to Lincoln during his debates with Douglas. The 14 December issue of Wilkes's Spirit of the Times, *for example, prints only a Lincolnless dialogue: "By George, I must shoot you; I made a vow that I would kill any man uglier than myself." "Fire away, stranger; if I'm uglier than you I don't want to live" (5:231). Haycraft's yarn opens with Lincoln "splitting rails with only shirt and breeches on" when a man armed with a gun tells him to look up.*

Says Lincoln What do you mean, the man replied that he had promised to shoot the first man he met who was uglier than himself—Lincoln asked to see the man's face and after taking a look remarked—If I am uglier then you, then blaze away—opening his shirt bosom.[11]

14 OCTOBER. From his nomination, Lincoln had to contend with persistent pests pursuing government posts. The South, a Baltimore newspaper, reprinted an incident from a Philadelphia newspaper and added a disclaimer: "The jest is so much in the President's well known style, that no one can doubt its authenticity. We are only surprised that one of his friends should have seen fit to give it to the world."

Lincoln took [the office seeker] aside, and the politician . . . thought he would go home with his commission. But the President merely said to him, My dear sir, before I left Springfield, Illinois, I had in my pig sty a little bit of a pig, that made a terrible commotion—do you know why? Because the old sow had just one more little pig than she had teats, and the little porker that got no teat made a terrible squealing.[12]

1862

10 JANUARY. With so many other failures to worry about, Lincoln was particularly frustrated by General George B. McClellan's inertia at Manassas. When McClellan, ill with typhoid fever, refused to see him, Lincoln called Army of the Potomac generals William B. Franklin and Irvin McDowell to a council of war. McDowell noted how stress failed to dull the president's satiric edge.

The President said he was in great distress, and, as he had been to General McClellan's house, and the General did not ask to see him, and as he must talk to somebody, he had sent for General Franklin and myself, to obtain our opinion as to the possibility of soon commencing active operations with the Army of the Potomac. To use his own expression, if something was not soon done, the bottom would be out of the whole affair; and, if General McClellan did not want to use the army, he would like to "borrow it," provided he could see how it could be made to do something.[13]

28 JANUARY. New Yorker George Templeton Strong, who kept a diary for more than forty years, interviewed the president on affairs of the Sanitary Commission. In his diary, he tried to record the sound of

*Lincoln telling one of his celebrated stories to a cultivated New Yorker.
The president was explaining his attitude toward freeing slaves.*

He told us a lot of stories. Something was said about the pressure of the extreme anti-slavery party in Congress and in the newspapers for legislation about the status of all slaves. "Wa-al," says Abe Lincoln, "that reminds me of a party of Methodist parsons that was travelling in Illinois when I was a boy thar, and had a branch to cross that was pretty bad-ugly to cross, ye know, because the waters was up. And they got considerin' and discussin' how they should git across it, and they talked about it for two hours, and one on 'em thought they had ought to cross one way when they got there, and another another way, and they got quarrellin' about it, till at last an old brother put in, and he says, says he, 'Brethren, this here talk ain't no use. I never cross a river until I come to it.'"[14]

30 JULY. The Crisis *of Columbus, Ohio, reported Lincoln telling an old jest book favorite that Horace Porter later said the president had used as a comment on relations with England.*[15]

A distinguished officer was at Washington, and in an interview introduced the question of Emancipation. "Well, you see," said Mr. Lincoln, "we've got to be mighty cautious how we manage the nigger question. If we're not, we shall be like the barber out in Illinois, who was shaving a fellow with a hatchet face and lantern jaws like mine. The barber put his finger in the customer's mouth, to make his cheek stick out; but while shaving away he cut through the fellow's cheek and cut off his own finger. If we don't play smart about the nigger we shall do as the barber did."[16]

MAY. Thirty-year-old Edward Dicey, erudite and sophisticated traveling correspondent for London's Spectator *and* Macmillan's *Magazine, spent six months in the federal states and an afternoon in the company of Lincoln, which he described in the May 1862 issue of* Macmillan's. *In a popular book of his travels the following year, Dicey expanded the narrative with commentary and additional anecdotes Lincoln told in his presence or he had reasons to believe were authentic in contrast to "the almost incredible manner in which stories are coined about Mr. Lincoln. . . . He is a humorist, not a buffoon."*[17]

He has a rich fund of dry, Yankee humour, not inconsistent, as in the case of the nation itself, with a sort of habitual melancholy. . . . There are, perhaps, one or two Lincolniana which I may fairly quote, and which will show the style of his conversation. Some of the party began smoking, and

Mr. Seward, who was present, remarked laughingly, "I have always wondered how any man could ever get to be President of the United States with so few vices. The President, you know, I regret to say, neither drinks nor smokes." "That," answered the President, "is a doubtful compliment. I recollect once being outside a stage in Illinois, and a man sitting by me offered me a cigar. I told him I had no vices. He said nothing, smoked for some time, and then grunted out, 'It's my experience in life that folks who have got no vices have plaguey few virtues.'" [223]

A gentleman happened to tell how a friend of his had been expelled from New Orleans as a Unionist, and how, on his expulsion, when he asked to see the writ by which he was expelled, the deputation, which brought him the notice to quit, told him that the Confederate Government had made up their minds to do nothing unconstitutional, and so they had issued no illegal writ, but simply meant *to make* him go of his own free will. "Well," said Mr. Lincoln, "that reminds me of an hotel-keeper down at St. Louis, in the cholera time, who boasted that he had never had a death in his hotel. And no more he had, for, whenever a guest was dying in his house, he carried him out in his bed and put him in the street to die." At another time, the conversation turned upon the discussions as to the Missouri Compromise, and elicited the following quaint remark from the President;—"It used to amuse me some to find that the slaveholders wanted more territory because they had not room enough for their slaves, and yet they complained of not having the slave-trade because they wanted more slaves for their room." [224–25]

Shortly after [Simon] Cameron's resignation, an old acquaintance called upon the President, and, after American fashion, asked him point-blank why, when he turned out the Secretary of War, he did not get rid of the whole Cabinet. "Well, you know," was the answer, "there was a farmer, far West, whose fields were infested with skunks, so he set a trap and caught nine; he killed the first, but that made such an infernal stench that he thought he had better let the rest go." [225]

24 MAY. A month earlier James Shields, now a general, had repulsed Stonewall Jackson in the Shenandoah Valley but, being wounded, could not pursue him. Admiral John Dahlgren's diary shows how the reputation of Lincoln's rash old friend evoked an even older joke. In Joe Miller's Jests (1745) it had been about King George and General James Wolfe. Lincoln recycled the joke in an 1863 interview, with whiskey replacing madness and the king and Wolfe transformed into Lincoln and Grant.

About five o'clock A.M. the President came in from his room half dressed, and sat down between the Secretary [Stanton] and myself. He was reminded of a joke, at which we laughed heartily. . . . The President remarked that Shields was said to be crazy, which put him in mind that George III had been told the same of one of his generals, viz., that he was mad. The king replied he wished he would bite his other generals.[18]

11 JULY. The popular press used Lincoln as a bottomless resource for filler material even in Southern Punch, *which would repeat jokes in succeeding issues.*

Old Abe, in discussing the political polygamic interests of Utah, is said to have remarked: "It is all nonsense to talk about polygamy. I know, from experience, that one wife at a time is as much as any man can get along with."[19]

12 AUGUST. The New York Herald *reported how Lincoln reluctantly denied as against army regulations a wounded soldier's appeal to leave the hospital, go home, recruit, and lead a new company of recruits. He likened the absurd order to what would today be called a Catch-22.*

The President expressed deep sympathy for [the soldier], but declined to cut the red tape which binds our government together. He said, the Corporal's case is a hard one, and reminds me of a story told by Judge B., of Illinois, of the officers of some county town in Ireland, who met and resolved, First, to build a new jail; second, to build it out of the old one; and third, to keep the prisoners in the old jail till the new one was built. And thus the country loses the services of as brave a soldier as she has in her ranks, and a true man is kept caged in the hospital while panting to be in the field.[20]

1863

8 JANUARY. Jesse W. Fell, leading Illinois Republican and long a Lincoln supporter, was instrumental in nominating Lincoln for president. He passed on to Chicago city attorney John Lyle King, an old Indiana Whig, a joke told by Joseph A. Wright, former conservative governor of that state who the following week would be sent to the U.S. Senate as a Unionist. Mrs. Lincoln had posed in Matthew Brady's New York studio in February 1861 draped in a glamorous, billowing evening gown. The inscription on the back was Brady's copyright notice.

Mr. Fell who sat at table with me yesterday told me of Old Abe's last joke. Mrs. Lincoln had her *card de visite* taken in New York, Brady had multiplied or manifolded them and they were stamped on the back "entered by Act of Congress." She sent him one in a letter, which he opened and looked at, and seeing the inscription remarked, in his way, "That's a lie— she never was entered by 'Act of Congress.'" Gov. Wright of Indiana was the repeater to Fell of the joke.[21]

19 SEPTEMBER. The popular Frank Leslie's Illustrated Newspaper, *celebrating the president as "the Aesop of the new world," fathered a timely fable upon him. The National Conscription Act passed in early March, but records show no protest from "a little village in Illinois." Even if apocryphal, this tale heralds the surge of orphan anecdotes the popular press attached to the president.*

On a recent occasion a deputation from a little village in Illinois called upon him to complain about the draft. He told them that he thought they were more frightened than hurt and offered as consolation this pleasant illustration: There is this little one horse village in Maryland, whose quota of the conscription was one man. When the enrolling officer went round to the farmhouses to get the names he was very solemn in his injunction to the old woman to give the name of every male creature on the farm among whom there was one called Billy Bray. When the drafting came round the lot fell upon the unfortunate Billy Bray. In due time the Provost Marshal came for his valuable conscript, and it proved Billy Bray was the farmer's donkey. "So," said Lincoln, "gentlemen you may be the donkey of your town and escape. Therefore don't disturb yourselves by meeting troubles half way."[22]

18 JULY—23 DECEMBER. John Hay's diary recorded stories and bon mots that Lincoln told in the White House, as in explaining why he avoided the death penalty in courts-martial: "He said it would frighten the poor devils too terribly to shoot them." Some entries are self-sustaining scenarios of stories reconstructed by others as cataloged in Zall's Abe Lincoln Laughing. *Referring to the following hog-stealer story, Hay's modern editor, Michael Burlingame, notes that Lincoln allegedly offered the same advice in a murder trial.*[23]

One fellow who had deserted and escaped after conviction into Mexico, he sentenced, saying "We will condemn him as they used to sell hogs in Indiana, as they run." [64]

He told one devilish good story about U[sher] F. Linder, getting a fellow off who had stolen a hog, by advising him to go and get a drink and suggesting that the water was better in Tennessee, etc. etc. [64]

The President said the Army dwindled on a march like a shovelfull of live fleas being pitched from one place to another. [76]

In a letter to his friend Charles Graham Halpine, humor columnist for the New York Post, *John Hay expanded on this entry: "An infernal nuisance named Lincoln Postmaster at Brooklyn fastened himself to the Tycoon the other day and Honest Abraham quickly put him off with a story of his friend Jesse Dubois, who, being State Auditor, had control of the State House at Springfield, Ill. An itinerant quack preacher wanted the use of the Representatives Hall to deliver a religious lecture. 'What's it about' said Jesse. 'The Second Coming of Christ' said the parson. 'Nonsense' roared Uncle Jesse, 'If Christ had been to Springfield once, and got away, he'd be damned clear of coming again.' This won't do for you to repeat, being blasphemous and calculated to hurt the 'Quaker vote.' I charge you not to use it."—But Halpine did use it, 17 February 1864.[24]*

The Second Coming. If J.C. had ever been to Springfield once he would [never] come again. [77]

The next entry refers to an often repeated anecdote expanded in Henry J. Raymond's authoritative Life and Public Services of Abraham Lincoln *(1865), 720–21:*

[Raymond told him that Secretary of the Treasury Chase was running for president.] Mr. Lincoln said he did not much concern himself about that. It was very important to him and the country that the department over which his rival presided should be administered with vigor and energy, and whatever would stimulate the Secretary to such action would do good. "Raymond," said he, "you were brought up on a farm, were you not? then you know what a chin-fly is. My [step]brother and I," he added, "were once ploughing corn on a Kentucky farm, I driving the horse and he holding plough. The horse was lazy, but on one occasion rushed across the field so that I, with my long legs could scarcely keep pace with him. On reaching the end of the furrow, I found an enormous chin-fly fastened upon him, and knocked him off. My brother asked me what I did that for. I told him I didn't want the old horse bitten in that way. 'Why,' said my brother, 'that's all that made him go.' Now," said Mr. Lincoln, "if Mr. Chase has a presidential chin-fly biting him, I'm not going to knock him off, if it will only make his department go."

The Presidential aspirations of Mr [Salmon P.] Chase are said to have been compared by the President to a horsefly on the neck of a plough-horse—which kept him lively about his work. [78]

[Thomas] Corwin's story about the advertising pulpit [in which the preacher advertises] "fine powder at Bill Smithers"—and an indignant Auditor's reply Taint wuth a damn—grains big as rat t[ur]ds—and I would walk through hell with a bag full of it. [78]

Today [September 29] came to the Executive Mansion an assembly of cold-water men and cold-water women to make a temperance speech . . . in which they called Intemperance the cause of our defeats. He could not see it, as the rebels drink more and worse whiskey than we do. [89]

Tonight the President said he was much relieved at hearing from [General John] Foster that there was firing at Knoxville yesterday. He said anything showing [General Ambrose] Burnside was not overwhelmed was cheering: Like Sallie Carter when she heard one of her children squall would say "There goes one of my young uns, not dead yet, bless the Lord." [118]

Lincoln probably told the next anecdote about a quack doctor plaintiff being cross-examined in his suit to recover surgical fees, as in David Paul Brown's sketch in The Forum *(1856), 2:375–76, with such exchanges as:*

Counsel.—"Did you decapitate him?"
　　Witness.—"Undoubtedly I did—that was a matter of course."
　　Counsel.—"Did you perform the Caesarean operation upon him?"
　　Witness.—"Why, of course, his condition required it."

Tonight the President talking with [Isaac N.] Arnold and me, told a magnificent Western law story about a steam doctor's Bill. [124]

The President tonight had a dream. He was in a party of plain people and as it became known who he was they began to comment on his appearance. One of them said, "He is a very common-looking man." The President replied "The Lord prefers Common-looking people: that is the reason he makes so many of them." [132]

12 AUGUST. General Francis P. Blair Jr., brother of Postmaster General Montgomery Blair and a member of Congress, reported to the military commander of Missouri, General John M. Scholfield, on a conversation with the president. Schofield was being harassed by Missouri politicians as well as insurgents. The next year Lincoln would greet him with, "I haven't heard anything against you for a year."[25]

He said in regard to the Guerillas in Lafayette and Jackson counties of whom you propose to dispose and at the same time remove the causes of their organization, that his position could be very well illustrated by an anecdote. An Irishman once asked for a glass of soda water and remarked at the same time that he would be glad if the Doctor could put a little brandy in it *"unbeknownst to him."* The inference is that old Abe would be glad if you would dispose of the Guerillas and would not be sorry to see the negroes set free, if it can be done without his being known in the affair as having instigated it. He will be certain to recognize it afterward as a military necessity.[26]

30 OCTOBER. A delegation from Kansas and Missouri had met with the president in September demanding immediate emancipation and also removal of General Schofield as military commander. In mid-October Lincoln rejected the demands in an open letter. The St. Louis Democrat *replied with an anecdote of its own.*

The secret of the President's policy in thus dodging the issues . . . has been related by himself, and in his own characteristic way—by anecdote. . . . He remarked that he had adopted the plan learned when a farmer boy engaged in plowing. When he came across stumps too deep and too tough to be torn up, and too wet to burn, he plowed around them. The President's reply, all the way through, shows evidence of plowing round the stumps.[27]

19 NOVEMBER. The Salem, Illinois, Advertiser *joked about the long-range consequences of the president's humor.*

Two Quaker ladies were discussing the probable termination of the war. "I think," said the first, "that Jefferson Davis will succeed."
    "Why does thee think so?"

"Because Jefferson is a praying man."

"And so is Abraham."

"Yes, but the Lord will think Abraham is joking."[28]

15 DECEMBER. A Chicago Tribune correspondent reported Lincoln's jocular remark about his breaking out with a light form of smallpox. Within a few days, the remark appeared in both George Templeton Strong's diary and a letter by Maine's senator, William P. Fessenden. Two months later the New York Post improved the punch line to read "I've got something now that I can give to everybody."

Since he has been president, he has always had a crowd of people asking him to give them something, but . . . now he has something he can give them all.[29]

19 DECEMBER. Samuel L. M. Barlow, New York powerbroker in the Democratic Party, repeated a Lincoln quip to at least two correspondents: "Dear Joe" and "My dear Dillan." The letter to Dillan identified the setting as Washington's F. Street Hospital and the lady as "Miss Howe of Boston." The episode would later surface in the Democrats' campaign jest book of 1864, Lincolniana, or the Humours of Uncle Abe.[30]

I have just heard the following story of our President, which may amuse you. He went with a young woman to a Soldiers Hospital in Washington, where she became much interested in the condition of a young man and the following conversation ensued.

Lady: Where were you wounded?

Soldier: At Antietam.

Lady: Yes, but *where* were you wounded?

Soldier: At Antietam.

Lady: But how were you wounded?

Soldier: At Antietam.

Lady then begs the President to help her as she feels a deep interest in the poor Soldier.

President. My good man, where were you wounded?

Soldier: At Antietam.

President. Where did the ball hit you.

Soldier. It passed through my testicles.

President rejoins the young lady who asks, "Well, Mr. President have you found how the man was wounded."

32

President: Yes, at Antietam.

Lady: But where was he struck?

President: Taking young lady by both hands, affectionately, "My dear Girl, the ball that *hit* him, would have *missed* you."[31]

1864

T. R. Dawley, "Publisher for the Millions," this year issued The President Lincoln Campaign Songster *along with multiple editions of* Old Abe's Jokes, *a cesspool of apocrypha, with clippings from the popular press, such as the following, that defy authentication.*

A western correspondent writes: "A visitor, congratulating Mr. Lincoln on the prospects of his re-election, was answered by that indefatigable story-teller with an anecdote of an Illinois farmer, who undertook to blast his own rocks. His first effort at producing an explosion proved a failure. He explained the cause by exclaiming, 'Pshaw, this powder has been shot before.'" [103]

When Mrs. [Clement] Vallandigham left Dayton to join her husband [in exile], just before the election, she told her friends that she expected never to return until she did so as the wife of the Governor of Ohio. Mr. Lincoln is said to have got off the following:—"That reminds me of a pleasant little affair that occurred out in Illinois. A gentleman was nominated for Supervisor. On leaving home on the morning of the election, he said—'Wife, tonight you shall sleep with the Supervisor of this town.' The election passed, and the confident gentleman was defeated. The wife heard the news before her defeated spouse returned home. She immediately dressed for going out, and waited her husband's return, when she met him at the door. 'Wife, where are you going at this time of night?' he exclaimed. 'Going?' she replied, 'why, you told me this morning that I should tonight sleep with the Supervisor of this town, and as Mr. L. is elected instead of yourself, I was going to his house.'" [47]

One entry has Lincoln retooling an ancient fable originally about frogs frightening an entire village. George Boutwell said he heard the president tell it about Irishmen in the May Republican convention at Cleveland that nominated Fremont instead of Lincoln. Lincoln did not attend. Frank B. Carpenter merely said Lincoln told it to him. Benjamin Cowen said he told it referring to Fremont's campaign. Ward Lamon repeatedly said he told it with reference to censorship.[32]

[A visitor said rumors that Ohio prefers Salmon P. Chase to Lincoln "all amounted to nothing."] At this announcement the President seemed well pleased and rubbing his hands, he exclaimed, "That reminds me of a story. Some years ago two Irishmen landed in this country, and taking the way out into the interior after labor, came suddenly near a pond of water, and to their great horror they heard some bull-frogs singing their usual song—Baum!—Baum!—Baum! They listened and trembled, and feeling the necessity of bravery they clutched their shellalies and crept cautiously forward, straining their eyes in every direction to catch a glimpse of the enemy, but he was not to be found. At last a happy idea came to the most forward one and he sprang to his mate, and exclaimed, 'and sure, Jamie, it is my opinion it's nothing but a noise.'" [121]

2 FEBRUARY. A trustworthy resource, the diary of Secretary of the Navy Gideon Welles, records a story Lincoln told in a cabinet meeting about interfering when Spain reannexed Santo Domingo. They would anger Spain if they did, American abolitionists if they did not.

The dilemma reminded him of the interview between two Negroes, one of whom was a preacher endeavoring to admonish and enlighten the other. "There are," said Josh, the preacher, "two roads for you, Joe. Be careful which you take. One ob dem leads straight to hell; de odder go right to damnation." Joe opened his eyes under the impressive eloquence and awful future and exclaimed, "Josh, take which road you please; I go troo de wood." I am not disposed [continued the president] to take any new trouble just at this time and shall neither go for Spain nor the Negro in this matter, but shall take to the woods.[33]

11 FEBRUARY. Charles Hale, a thirty-three-year-old editor of the Boston Daily Advertiser, *wrote to his brother from Washington about the president using stories as delaying tactics. His informants were Senator Ben Wade of Ohio and Schuyler Colfax, Speaker of the House.*

—At a dinner at Alley's day before yesterday Ben Wade of Ohio, apropos of President Lincoln's stories said "When we were urging the President up to the Emancipation Proclamation, he asked me one day if I remembered a picture in the Esop's fables we used to have at school, of the negro in a tub, and men trying in vain to wash him white. 'Now, (said the President) that's just the idle job you want me to undertake.'" —I remarked that still the President all the time that he talked in that way, (of which you know we have many illustrations) must have really determined in the bottom of his mind to make the Emancipation Proclamation, and wished to bother his interlocutors; to veil his purpose; to see what arguments they would use, etc. Colfax (here is the point) said that is so; that the President had showed him (Colfax) the genuine article of the Emancipation Proclamation which he (Lincoln) prepared as early as July 17, 1862, a little more than two months before the actual issue, from which it differed but slightly.[34]

17 FEBRUARY. The New York Post's *page 1 featured nearly two columns of "Several Little Stories by or about President Lincoln." Most of the stories were recycled from gossip or earlier newspapers and periodicals. The few items below were probably transmitted from the White House by John Hay. The opposition, the* New York Herald, *taunted the* Post *by reprinting the "Several Little Stories." Though Republican, the* Post *did not relish the president's reelection, so the* Herald *captioned the stories "The Presidential Campaign: The First Electioneering Document. The Evening Post Out in Favor of 'Old Abe.'"[35]*

Mr. Lincoln, as the highest public official of the nation, is necessarily very much bored by all sorts of people calling upon him. An officer of the government called one day at the White House, and introduced a clerical friend. "Mr. President," said he, "allow me to present to you my friend, the Rev. Mr. F. of ——. Mr. F. has expressed a desire to see you and have some conversation with you, and I am happy to be the means of introducing him." The President shook hands with Mr. F. and, desiring him to be seated, took a seat himself. Then—his countenance having assumed an expression of patient waiting—he said, "I am now ready to hear what you have to say." "O bless you, sir," said Mr. F., "I have nothing especially to say. I merely called to pay my respects to you, and, as one of the million, to assure you of my hearty sympathy and support." "My dear sir," said the President, rising promptly—his face showing instant relief, and with both hands grasping that of his visitor, "I am very glad to see you; I am very glad to see you indeed! *I thought you had come to preach to me!*"

Similar to the next item, analogues about Lincoln's telling jokes amid serious discussions surface in recollections by James Ashley, Isaac Arnold, and William Herndon. Ashley reported Lincoln's saying, "If I couldn't tell these stories, I would die."[36]

Another member of Congress was conversing with the President, and was somewhat annoyed by the President's propensity to divert attention from the serious subject he had in mind by ludicrous allusions. "Mr. Lincoln," said he, "I think you would have your joke if you were within a mile of hell." "Yes," said the President, "that is about the distance to the Capitol."

> *The next item refers to a scandal the previous year. John Mosby's raiders caught General E. H. Stoughton asleep on a Sunday morning at Fairfax Courthouse. He was supposed to be searching for Mosby. General Benjamin Butler recalled Lincoln spoke of a sleeping young lieutenant who would cost as much as sixteen horses.[37]*

When informed that General Stoughton had been captured by the rebels at Fairfax, the President is reported to have said that he did not mind the loss of the brigadier as much as he did the loss of the horses. "For," said he, "I can make a much better brigadier in five minutes, but the horses cost a hundred and twenty-five dollars a piece."

Mr. Lincoln has a very effective way sometimes of dealing with men who trouble him with questions. Somebody asked him how many men the rebels had in the field. He replied very seriously, "Twelve hundred thousand, according to the best authority." The interrogator blanched in the face, and ejaculated, "My God!" "Yes, sir, twelve hundred thousand—no doubt of it. You see, all of our Generals, when they get whipped, say the enemy outnumbers them from three to five to one, and I must believe them. We have four thousand men in the field, and three times four make twelve. Don't you see it?" The inquisitive man looked for his hat after "seeing it."

> *21 FEBRUARY. In reminiscing about the president, Noah Brooks later noted, "He used to say that the grim grotesqueness and extravagance of American humor were its most striking characteristic."[38] The example now is from the* New York Herald *telling how Lincoln, visiting a military hospital, saw a wounded soldier laughing at a religious tract handed him by a lady.*

The President said, "The lady doubtless means you well, and it's hardly fair for you to laugh at her gift." "Well, Mr. President," replied the soldier, "she has given me a tract on the 'Sin of Dancing' and both my legs are shot off."

> *16 MAY. Supplementing T. R. Dawley's commercial joke books, New York Democrats compiled a joke book of their own for the presidential campaign,* Lincolniana, or the Humors of Uncle Abe, *dating the preface as from Springfield, 1 April, to signify satire. The most recent joke*

is dated 16 May, as if claiming to be fresh and timely, but most entries are recycled from previous publications or malicious mockery—like the repulsive anecdote alleged to be from Lincoln that names actual old friends.

I attended court many years ago at Mt. Pulaski, the first county seat of Logan County, and there was the jolliest set of rollicking young Lawyers there that you ever saw together. There was Bill F[ickli]n, Bill H[erndo]n, L[eonard] S[wet]t, and a lot more, and they mixed Law and Latin, water and whisky, with equal success. It so fell out that the whisky seemed to be possessed of the very spirit of Jonah. At any rate, S[wet]t went out to the hog-pen, and, leaning over, began to "throw up Jonah." The hogs evidently thought it feed time, for they rushed forward and began to squabble over the voided matter. "Don't fight (hic)," said S[wet]t, "there's enough (hic) for all." [55]

Lincoln told the next story in response to rumors that Salmon P. Chase would resign as secretary of the Treasury to run for president. Later memoirists A. T. Rice and F. F. Browne concur that Lincoln told the story to the messenger bringing news of Fredericksburg, 13 December 1862. Rice said a hog pursued the boys, and Browne said it was a dog. Harper's New Monthly Magazine *(June 1865) did not mention Lincoln and said the treed boy's companion was named John and their antagonist was a bear.[39]*

It is not so easy a thing to let Chase go. I am situated very much as the boy who held the bear by the hind legs. I will tell you how it was. There was a very vicious bear which, after being some time chased by a couple of boys, turned upon his pursuers. The boldest of the two ran up and caught the bear by the hind legs, while the other climbed up into a little tree, and complacently witnessed the conflict going on beneath, between the bear and his companion. The tussle was a sharp one, and the boy, after becoming quite exhausted, cried out in alarm, "Bill, for God's sake come down and help me let this darned bear go!" [74]

The next Lincolniana entry's style is far below Lincoln's efforts at dialect, but the substance is authenticated by Goldwin Smith's diary for 16 November 1864 that mentions Lincoln's story of "the three pigeons." Smith paraphrased the story (without dialect) in MacMillan's Magazine, *February 1865.[40] The story was a favorite of the jest books. The* American Jest Book *(Philadelphia, 1789) gave the punch line to the mathematician.*

There was a darkey in my neighborhood, called Pompey, who, from a certain quickness in figuring up the prices of chickens and vegetables, got the reputation of being a mathematical genius. Johnson, a darkey preacher, heard of Pompey, and called to see him. "Here ye're a great mat'm'tishum, Pompey." "Yes sar, you jas try." . . . "Now, Pompey, spose dere am tree pigeons sittin' on a rail fence, and you fire a gun at 'em and shoot one, how many's left?" "Two, ob coors," replies Pompey after a little wool scratching. "Ya-ya-ya," laughs Mr. Johnson, "I knowed you was a fool, Pompey; dere's none left—one's dead, and d'udder two's flown away." [77]

The final sample from Lincolniana *relates to the 20 February "massacre at Olustee" in which 300 out of 350 black troops were killed in a campaign initiated when the president made John B. Hay of Illinois a major (not to be confused with Lincoln's secretary), in order to carry suggestions to the Florida command. When someone who knew Hay regretted the assignment, the president here responds with a popular story about a Hoosier. The story with no mention of Lincoln had appeared in the 1842* Old American Comic Almanac *of Boston and more recently in* Leslie's Illustrated Newspaper *for 26 November 1859.*

"About Hay," said Uncle Abe, "the fact was, I was pretty much like John Hawks, out in Illinois, who sold a dog to a hunting neighbor, as a first-rate coon dog. A few days after, the fellow brought him back, saying he 'wasn't worth a cuss for coons.' 'Well,' said Jim, 'I tried him for everything else, and he wasn't worth a d—n, and so I thought he must be good for coons.'" (65)

22 MAY. John Hay's diary recorded his own estimate of General Benjamin Butler as "perfectly useless and incapable of campaigning," quarreling with other generals and being a regular nuisance. When he said, "Butler was the only man in the army in whom power would be dangerous," the president concurred.

"Yes . . . he is like Jim Jett's brother Jim used to say that his brother was the damdest scoundrel that ever lived but in the infinite mercy of Providence he was also the damdest fool."[41]

1 JULY. Samuel Wilkeson, head of the New York Tribune's *Washington bureau, supported Lincoln's reelection but called him "the border-state joking machine." Wilkeson chafed so badly under attempts to censor*

*war correspondents that he ordered his staff to join the army, thereby
embedding reporters with the troops. On 1 July he wrote that Salmon P.
Chase resigned because Lincoln had subverted "the purity" of the Treasury Department and impugned Chase's "personal integrity."[42] When
John Hay offered to reply with the facts, the president reminded him of
a story he also told F. B. Carpenter about the father's response to his
boy who warned about "wrigglers" in the cheese.[43]*

This evening I referred to Wilkeson's blackguardedly misstatements
in today's Tribune and asked if I might not prepare a true statement of
facts to counteract the effects of these falsehoods; he answered "Let 'em
wriggle."[44]

*22 DECEMBER. Joseph Medill, part owner and Washington correspon-
dent of the* Chicago Tribune, *gave the Republican Party its name and
helped engineer Lincoln's election yet often railed in person and in
print against his timorous policies. During an interview printed in the*
Tribune *on Christmas Day, Medill commented on the defeat of J. B.
Hood's forty-five thousand men in Tennessee: "Hood's army, as a military organization, is pretty effectually destroyed"—an expression that
triggered a down-home story that Lincoln told him and repeated to
others.[45] Although he had been friends with Lincoln for over a decade,
Medill stumbled on Lincoln's dialect, such as "yellar dorg."*

"The present condition of Hood's army reminds me of the story of Bill
Syke's dog. Did you ever hear it?"

"No, I don't think I did."

"Well, the thing happened down below Beardstown on the Illinois
River a good many years ago. Sykes owned a long-legged, wolfish 'yellar'
dog that was in the habit of prowling about and breaking into the neighbors' meat houses, killing sheep, and committing other depredations.
People had tried to shoot and poison him, but somehow they failed to
dispatch the brute. At last a neighbor, named John Henderson, concluded
he would try an experiment on him. The dog had plundered his milk
house, eaten his cream, and upset the crocks of milk. So he took a coon's
bladder, which one of his boys had dried, filled it with powder, scooped
out the soft part of a biscuit, slipped in the bag of powder, and when the
dog next came in sight he stuck a piece of punk in the mouth of the bladder, set fire to it, closed up the biscuit with butter, and laid it down. In a
minute, the 'dorg' came along, smelled the bread, and gobbled it down at
a single gulp. 'All right,' says Henderson, 'we shall soon see how things

will work.' In a minute or two there was a tremendous explosion, as if a torpedo had gone off under one of our gunboats. The head of the 'yaller dorg' rolled down the hill; the hind legs flew some distance, catching on a fence stake; the fore quarters fell on the porch; and the intestines scattered around on the ground for a couple of rods.

"'Well,' says a neighbor who happened to come along, 'I guess you have got rid of that cussed dog at last?' 'Yes,' says Henderson, 'I reckon that *that* dog, *as a dog,* won't be of much account hereafter.' So with Hood's army; I reckon that *that* army, *as an army,* won't be of much account hereafter."[46]

1865

23 MARCH. A reporter for the American and Commercial Advertiser *of Baltimore recorded the president's comments to typical visitors and office-seekers parading through his office two days earlier.*

[To an old man who came to Washington hoping for employment:] Washington was the worst place in the country for anyone to seek to better their condition. He wished some species of saffron tea could be administered to produce an eruption of those already in Washington and make this migration fever strike out instead of striking in.

[To a young war widow hoping to be named a small town postmistress:] Although he was president, she must remember that he was but one horse in the team, and if the others pulled in a different direction, it would be a hard matter for him to out-pull them.

[To someone hoping to avoid conscription:] If I were, by interfering, to make a hole through which a kitten might pass, it would soon be large enough for the old cat to get through also.[47]

CHAPTER 3

STORIES TOLD AFTER APRIL 1865 BY THOSE WHO KNEW LINCOLN WELL

1865

31 MAY. Following Lincoln's funeral, New York Times *editor Henry J. Raymond worked feverishly to write a complete biography superior to his 1864 campaign biography. The new* Life and Public Services of Abraham Lincoln *boasted eight hundred pages, of which painter Francis N. Carpenter supplied seventy-five pages of "Anecdotes and Reminiscences of President Lincoln," a timely resource for newspapers. Carpenter retold many stories he said he had heard during the six months he painted Lincoln reading the draft of the Emancipation Proclamation. He also repeated stories from friends and some from the press. As Don and Virginia Fehrenbacher found, "It is not always easy to tell the difference."[1] Suspicious of his sources and his style, I nevertheless sample Carpenter's stories that lie within the outer limits of probability. An example of a contemporary eyewitness disputing Carpenter's reports would be the Augusta, Georgia,* Chronicle and Sentinel *for 7 June reporting a dialogue between Lincoln and the British arbitrator R.M.T. Hunter at the Hampton Roads peace conference.*

Mr. Hunter made a long reply, insisting that the recognition of [Jefferson] Davis's power to make a treaty was the first and indispensable step to peace, and referring to the correspondence between King Charles the First and his Parliament, as a reliable precedent of a constitutional ruler treating with rebels. Mr. Lincoln's face then wore that indescribable expression which generally preceded his hardest hits, and he remarked, "Upon questions of history I must refer you to Mr. Seward, for he is posted on such things, and I don't profess to be bright. My only distinct recollection of the matter is, that Charles lost his head."[2]

More controversial, Carpenter's version concluded with the farmer saying, "Well, it may come pretty hard on their snouts, but I don't see but that it will be 'root, hog, or die!'" Alexander Stephens, an old friend but vice president of the Confederacy, had been at the conference and insisted that the newspaper version given here was more accurate.[3]

Mr. Hunter said something about the inhumanity of leaving so many poor old negroes and young children destitute by encouraging the able-bodied negroes to run away, and asked, what are they—the helpless—to do? Mr. Lincoln said that reminded him of an old friend in Illinois, who had a crop of potatoes, and did not want to dig them. So he told a neighbor that he would turn in his hogs and let them dig them for themselves. "But," said the neighbor, "the frost will soon be in the ground, and when the soil is hard frozen, what will they do then?" To which the worthy farmer replied, "Let 'em root!"[4]

More reliable when corroborated are stories like the one about Daniel Webster that Lincoln later told to Byron Johnson, head of the Sunday School Union, while reviewing a parade of colored children on 31 May. Carpenter's version supplanted the one in Joe Miller's Jests *(1745), where it had been about a "Dr. Wall."*[5]

I heard a story last night about Daniel Webster when a lad, which was new to me, and it has been running in my head all the morning. When quite young, at school, Daniel was one day guilty of a gross violation of the rules. He was detected in the act, and called up by the teacher for punishment. This was to be the old-fashioned "feruling" of the hand. His hands happened to be very dirty. Knowing this, on his way to the teacher's desk he *spit* upon the palm of his *right* hand, wiping it off upon the side of his pantaloons. "Give me your hand, sir," said the teacher, very sternly. Out went the right hand, partly cleansed. The teacher looked at it a moment, and said, "Daniel, if you will find another hand in this school-room as filthy as that, I will let you off this time!" Instantly from behind his back came the *left* hand. "Here it is, sir," was the ready reply. "That will do," said the teacher, "for this time; you can take your seat, sir!"[6]

Carpenter quoted an oft-told story about Joseph Baldwin, author of the best-selling Flush Times of Alabama and Mississippi *(1853). In making the narrative more dramatic the story includes one suspect detail in calling Southerner Baldwin, who had died the previous year, "a good union man." The statement remained thus in Frank Moore's popular* Anecdotes, Poetry and Incidents of the War *(1866). Page references in brackets are to Carpenter's anecdotes in Henry J. Raymond's* Life and Public Services of Abraham Lincoln.

Judge Baldwin, of California, being in Washington, called one day on General Halleck, and, presuming upon a familiar acquaintance in California a few years since, solicited a pass outside of our lines to see a brother in Virginia, not thinking that he would meet with a refusal, as both his brother and himself were good Union men. "We have been deceived too often," said General Halleck, "and I regret I can't grant it." Judge B. then went to Stanton, and was very briefly disposed of with the same result. Finally he obtained an interview with Mr. Lincoln, and stated his case. "Have you applied to General Halleck?" inquired the President. "Yes, and met with a flat refusal," said Judge B. "Then you must see Stanton," continued the President. "I have, and with the same result," was the reply. "Well, then," said Mr. Lincoln, with a smile, "I can do nothing; for you must know *that I have very little influence with this Administration*." [747–48]

In an eyewitness report, Carpenter innocently has the president talk about Sar Kasem, a fictional character in Judge Baldwin's Flush Times: *"He might approve of a law making it death for a man to blow his nose in the street, but would be for rebelling if it allowed the indictment to dispense with stating in which hand he held it."*[7]

One evening the President brought a couple of friends into the "State dining-room" to see my [painting]. Something was said, in the conversation that ensued, that "reminded" him of the following circumstance: "Judge ——," said he, "held the strongest ideas of rigid government and close construction that I ever met. It was said of him, on one occasion, that he would hang a man for blowing his nose in the street, but he would quash the indictment if it failed to specify which hand he blew it with!" [753–54]

Primitive "mud-shallop," stern-wheel steamboats were plunging and wallowing on the Illinois River by 1848, giving Carpenter's yarn about Jack Chase a plausible setting.

During a public "reception," a farmer, from one of the border counties of Virginia, told the President that the Union soldiers, in passing his farm, had helped themselves not only to hay, but his horse, and he hoped the President would urge the proper officer to consider his claim immediately. Mr. Lincoln said that this reminded him of an old acquaintance of his, "Jack Chase," who used to be a lumberman on the Illinois, a steady, sober man, and the best raftsman on the river. It was quite a trick, twenty-five years ago, to take the logs over the rapids; but he was skilful with a raft, and always kept her straight in the channel. Finally a steamer was put on, and Jack was made Captain of her. He always used to take the wheel, going through the rapids. One day when the boat was plunging and wallowing along the boiling current, and Jack's utmost vigilance was being exercised to keep her in the narrow channel, a boy pulled his coat-tail, and hailed him with—"Say, Mister Captain! I wish you would just stop your boat a minute—I've lost my apple overboard!" [752–53]

In contrast to Carpenter's cut-and-pasted anecdotes, Henry J. Raymond's own recollections in the new book were based on frequent meetings and interviews covering Washington for the New York Times. *Carpenter said Lincoln called Raymond "my Lieutenant-General in politics," [758] and Raymond let it stand without correction. Raymond also gave popular currency to the story about the chin-fly that made his plow horse go [720] and another oft-quoted analogy about the pressures of being president.*

Much has been said of Mr. Lincoln's habit of telling stories, and it could scarcely be exaggerated. He had a keen sense of the humorous and the ludicrous, and relished jokes and anecdotes for the amusement they afforded him. But story-telling was with him rather a mode of stating and illustrating facts and opinions, than anything else. . . . Mr. Lincoln often gave clearness and force to his ideas by pertinent anecdotes and illustrations drawn from daily life. Within a month after his first accession to office, when the South was threatening civil war, and armies of office-seekers were besieging him in the Executive Mansion, he said to the writer of these pages that he wished he could get time to attend to the Southern question; he thought he knew what was wanted, and believed he could do something towards quieting the rising discontent; but the office-seekers demanded all his time. "I am," said he, "like a man so busy in letting rooms in one end of his house, that he can't stop to put out the fire that is burning the other." [720]

In May, William Herndon, Lincoln's law partner since 1843, began a two-year project to collect "facts and truths of his life—not fictions—not fables—not floating rumors, but facts—solid facts and well attested truths."[8] Interviewing old friends and family he collected testimonies from 250 informants of varying reliability as grist for the biographies that he would publish with collaborator Jesse Weik: Herndon's Lincoln: The True Story of a Great Life *(1889) and its revision in 1892. Enthralled by what would now be termed "psychobabble," he had trouble understanding Lincoln's humor. When Herndon asked his impression of Niagara Falls, Lincoln replied, "Where in the world did all that water come from?"—which Herndon took seriously.[9] His interviews by mail or in person generally followed a questionnaire with queries about intimate details like his health, reading and eating habits (e.g., Did he eat apples from the long end?), even sex life (Did he suffer from a socially transmitted disease?). He repeatedly asked them about Lincoln's celebrated storytelling.[10]*

29 MAY. William Herndon's cousin J. A. Herndon kept a store at New Salem with his brother J. Rowan Herndon, but knew Lincoln well only in Springfield. He passed on a comical speech Lincoln is supposed to have made at Pappsville in 1832. William Herndon printed a legible copy in the Illinois State Journal. *Postmaster Joseph Y. Ellis copied that and sent it back to him as a recollection.[11]*

Gentlemen and fellow citizens I presume you all Know who I am I am humble Abe Lincoln I have been solicited by many freinds to become a candidate for the Legislature. My politicks are short and sweet like the old Womans dance. I am in favor of a National bank. I am in favor of the internal improvement system and a high protective Tariff— These are my sentiments and politicle principles if Elected I shall be thankful if not it will be all the Same[12]

3 JULY. J. Rowan Herndon, who sold his share of his New Salem general store to Lincoln in 1832, referred to a political speech Lincoln made in that year and in the second anecdote referred to Bowling Green, Lincoln's benefactor and mentor at New Salem. Bracketed page numbers refer to Zall, Abe Lincoln Laughing.

As to his Indiana storys; he has told me many of them; there is one that he told me, about an old Baptist Preacher,— the meeting house was way off in the woods from any other house, and was only used once a month; this preacher was dessed in coarse linen pants, and shirt of the same material; the pants were made after the old fashion, with big bag legs and but one button to the waistbands, and two flap buttons, no suspenders; and the shirt had crimp sleeves and one button on the collar. He raised up in the Pulpit and took his Text, thus: I am the Christ whom I shall represent to-day; about this time one of these blue Lizards or scorpions ran up his legs; the old man began to slap away on his legs, but missed the Lizard, and kept getting higher up, he unbuttoned his pants at one snatch, and kicked off his pants, but the thing kept on up his back; the next motion was for the collar button of his shirt, and off it went. In the house was an old Lady, who took a good look at him, and said, well, if you represent Christ, I am done believing in the Bible. This anecdote he told somewhere in his speech, in reply to some of the opposite candidates, who had represented themselves something extra. [53]

He was once while living in Salem, called on by one Pete Lukins, to prove his character and standing as to the validity of his oath. The Attorney said, please state what you know as to the character of Mr. Lukins as for truth and veracity. Well, said Mr. Lincoln, he is called lying Pete Lukins. But said the Lawyer, would you believe him on oath. He turned round and said, ask Esquire [Bowling] Green—he has taken his testimony under oath many times. Green was asked the question and answered, I never believe anything he says unless somebody else swears the same thing. [53]

21 JULY. James W. Wartmann, a Rockport, Indiana, lawyer, relayed a story told by John W. Lamar, a schoolmate of Lincoln's. In later corroborating the story Lamar added that James Larkin, offended, wanted to fight, but "Lincoln looked as if he did not cear and told some kind of a joke that fit Larkins case and put the croud in a uproar of lafter and Larkin dride up." [54n]

Old Mr. Lamar (squire's father) was one day going to election—and I (squire L——) was on the horse behind him. We fell in company with an old man named James Larkin— this man Larkin was a great brag, always relating some miraculous story or other. While riding along we overtook Abe Lincoln going to the polls on foot. Old man Larkin commenced telling Lincoln about the great speed and "bottom" of the mare he was riding. Why, said Larkin, "Yesterday I run her *five* mile in *four* minutes, and she never drew a *long* breath." I guess, quietly replied Lincoln, She drew a great many *short ones*. [54]

3 AUGUST. Using Herndon's questionnaire, Nathaniel Branson, a lawyer of Petersburg, Illinois, interviewed James Short, one of Lincoln's best friends in New Salem and a political ally. The first anecdote sounds as if Lincoln had told a shaggy dog story. The second is about New Salem's leading merchant, quick-tempered Sam Hill. Lincoln succeeded Hill as postmaster of New Salem in 1833.[13]

Mr L. used to tell Mr S. the following anecdote of himself. Once, when Mr. L was surveying, he was put to bed in the same room with two girls, the head of his bed being next to the foot of the girls' bed. In the night he commenced tickling the feet of one of the girls with his fingers. As she seemed to enjoy it as much as he did he then tickled a little higher up; and as he would tickle higher the girl would shove down lower and the higher he tickled the lower she moved. Mr. L would tell the story with evident enjoyment. He never told how the thing ended.

He never got angry. Once when major Hill was wrongly informed that Mr. L had said something about his—H's—wife, the Major abused him a great deal for it—talking to Mr. L very roughly and insultingly. Mr. L kept his temper,—denied having said any thing against her.—told the Major that he had a very high opinion of her, and that if he knew any thing in the world against her it was the fact of her being his wife.[14]

Harper's New Monthly Magazine for July published a reminiscence by Noah Brooks, California newsman scheduled to be Lincoln's new secretary, who also testified that the president's wit cooled the heat.

Of a virulent personal attack upon his official conduct he mildly said that it was ill-timed; and of one of his most bitter political enemies [Congressman Henry W. Davis of Maryland] he said: "I've been told that insanity is hereditary in his family, and I think we will admit the plea in his case."[15]

SEPTEMBER. Herndon interviewed Joseph C. Richardson, who had known Lincoln back home in Indiana during the late 1820s. Richardson related an incident legendary in their neighborhood thanks to Lincoln's doggerel. The verse celebrated the practical joke Lincoln and friends played on the double-wedding night of Charles and Reuben Grigsby. After the brides were bedded, the boys were sent to the wrong rooms. Their mother, suspicious, double-checked. Alarmed, the boys bounced out of bed and came near knocking each other down. I have

*appended to Richardson's tale Lincoln's rendering as recollected in a
September interview by blind Elizabeth Crawford.*

—After the infair was ended the two women were put to bed. The candles
were blown out upstairs—the gentlemen—the two husbands were invited
and shown to bed. Chas. Grigsby got into bed with, *by an accident* as it
were, with Reuben Grigsby's wife and Reuben got into bed with Charles's
wife, by accident as it were. [Not having been invited to the wedding]
Lincoln, I say, was mortified and he declared that he would have revenge.
Lincoln was by nature witty and here was his chance. So he got up a witty
poem—called the Book of Chronicles in which the infair—the mistake
in partners . . . came in each for its share—and this poem is remembered here in Indiana in scraps better than the Bible—better than Watts'
Hymns. . . .

[*Scrap remembered by Elizabeth Crawford, aged sixty*] "I will tell you
a joke about Jouel and Mary; it is neither a joke or a story for Reuben and
Charles has married two girls, but Billy has married a boy.

> "The girls he had tried on every side
> But none could he get to agree;
> All was in vain, he went home again
> And since that, he is married to Natty.
>
> "So Billy and Natty agreed very well;
> And mammas well pleased at the match.
> The egg it is laid but Natty's afraid,
> The shell is so soft that it never will hatch.
>
> "But Betsey, she said: 'You cursed baldhead,
> My suitor you never can be,
> Besides your low crotch proclaims you a botch
> And that never can answer for me.'"[16]

1866

*23 JANUARY. Garrulous Abner Y. Ellis, postmaster at Springfield since
1849, supplied Herndon with a wealth of recollections old, new, borrowed, and blue. Two years earlier,* Harper's New Monthly Magazine
*(29 [Nov. 1864]: 820) had printed a California story about a lawyer
and a farmer arguing the merits of wine and whisky and almost coming to blows when the lawyer shouts, "Hold us, boys! Hold us! Two of
you hold him; one can hold me." It is hard to tell whether Ellis's adaptation was his own or Lincoln's.*

I am fearful that my selection of stories are not good and will be rather tiresome, so I will close with: Daddy can Hold me. Yes, Daddy can hold me. Two brave young men were going to fight, and were both stripping for the conflict, and both equally eager by all outward appearances to get together, but their friends interfered and were holding the most noisy one back; when he discovered his antagonist coming towards him, he said to his friends, Why don't some of you hold the other man! Daddy can hold me! Yes, Daddy, hold me, Daddy! For you know my temper! [57]

—How a bashful Young Man became a Married Man with 5 little bashful Boys, & How he and his red headed Wife became Millerites and before they wer to ascend [to Heaven] they agreed to make a clean breast of it to each other The old man insisted that the Wife should own up first as she had promised in her Marriage Vow to first obey her husband Well Dear said she, our little Sammy is not your child Well said the husband whoes is he Oh Dear said she; he is the one eyed shoe makers he came to see me once when you was away and in an evil hour I gave way. Well said the husband is the rest mine No said she they belong to the Neighbourhood Well said the old man I am ready to leave; *Gabarial blow your horn*. I have thought that Mr. L. had something to do with its getting up he used to tell it with embellishments. I suppose you have heard him telling it. he said he never saw a Millerite but what he thought of the story. [97–98]

Ellis's next anecdote plays a variation on Friar John's exemplum in Rabelais's Gargantua and Pantagruel, *book 4, chapter 67. English King Edward V teases French refugee François Villon with an image of the French coat of arms in the royal privy. Villon praises it as a cure for constipation—"For the very sight of them puts you into such a dreadful fright, that you immediately let fly."[17] More recently, an analogue had appeared on a scurrilous handbill dated 1864 substituting R. E. Lee for Washington and McClellan for the Englishman.[18]*

I once heard Mr. Lincoln tell an anecdote on Col. Ethan Allen of Revolutionary notoriety which I have never heard from any one besides him and for your amusement I will try and tell it as well as I can It appears that shortly after we had pease with England Mr. Allen had occasion to visit England, and while their the English took Great pleasure in teasing him, and trying to make fun of the Americans and General Washington in particular And one day they got a picture of General Washington, and hung it up the Back House where Mr Allen could see it And they finally asked Mr A. if he saw that picture of his friend in the Back House Mr Allen said No. but said he thought that it was a verry appropriate [place] for an Englishman to keep it Why they asked, for said Mr Allen their is Nothing that will make an Englishman SHIT so quick as the sight of Genl Washington And after that they let Mr Allens Washington alone.

3 MAY. Law student Charles Hart told Herndon that Lincoln had entertained Hart's parents with a down-home story probably during a public reception on 21 February 1863.

My father then remarked there were too many who wanted to be officers who are not suited to it, and Mr. Lincoln replied," Yes, it is so. That reminds me of a story I heard in a small town in Illinois where I once lived. Every man in town owned a fast horse, each one considering his own the fastest, so to decide the matter there was to be a trial of all the horses to take place at the same time. One old man living in the town known as "Uncle" was selected as umpire; when it was over and each one anxious for his decision, the old man putting his hands behind his back said "I have come to one conclusion, that where there are so many fast horses in our little town, none of them are any great shakes." [58]

12 OCTOBER. Herndon interviewed Caleb Carman a cobbler who met Lincoln building a flatboat at Sangamon Town and later was his landlord in New Salem. Carman said he could not remember any jokes about Abe but did offer a risible incident.

I saw Abe at a show one night at Sangamon town—upstairs at my uncle's— Jacob Carman; the Showman cooked eggs in Abe's hat—Abe, when the man called for the hat, said—"Mr., the reason I didn't give you my hat before was out of respect for your Eggs—not care for my hat." [58]

5 NOVEMBER. After an interview in Herndon's office, John B. Weber, a clerk in the state land records office, a friend, and a neighbor for thirty years, recorded an anecdote about Lincoln on a surveying trip. He was swapping stories with a Pennsylvanian who found it hard to believe from his appearance that he was a candidate for the legislature. Lincoln explained the situation to Weber with a joke that had been in the London jest book Royal Court Jester *in the 1790s.*

I will have to tell you an anecdote to give you some idea of the fix I was in before I was washed, but said I dont vouch for the truth of the anecdote.... In a village near where I lived, on a day when the weather was inclement and the roads exceedingly muddy, a toper named Bill got brutally drunk and staggered down a narrow alley where he layed himself down in the mud, and remained there until the dusk of the evening, at which time he recovered from his stupor; finding himself very muddy— immediately started for a pump (a public watering place on the street) to wash himself. On his way to the pump another drunken man was leaning over a horse post; this, Bill mistook for the pump and at once took hold of the arm of this man for the handle, the use of which set the occupant of the post to throwing up; Bill believing all was right put both hands under and gave himself a thorough washing. He then made his way to the grocery for something to drink. On entering the door one of his comrades exclaimed in a tone of surprise, Why, Bill, what in the world is the matter? Bill said in reply, I g[o]d you ought to have seen me before I was washed. [58–59]

25 NOVEMBER. John H. Wickizer, a Bloomington lawyer, responded to Herndon's appeal with an anecdote from the 1840s when Wickizer and Lincoln rode the Eighth Judicial Circuit together. An analogue in Harper's Weekly *(14 November 1857) told how an auctioneer complained to the wit Douglas Jerrold that business was going to the devil and received the same response.*

In 1858, in the Court at Bloomington, Illinois, Mr. Lincoln was engaged in a case of no very great importance, but the Attorney on the other side, Mr. S[cott], a young lawyer of fine abilities (now a judge) was always very sensitive about being beaten, and in this case manifested unusual zeal and interest. The case lasted till late at night, when it was finally submitted to the jury— Mr. S. spent a sleepless night in anxiety, and early next morning, learned to his great chagrin, he had lost the case. Mr. Lincoln met him at the Courthouse and asked him what had become of his case— with lugubrious countenance and melancholy tone, Mr. S. said "It's gone to h—l." "O well," said Mr. L., "then you'll see it again." [59]

11 DECEMBER. John H. Littlefield, who had been a law student under Lincoln and later made a portrait of him on his deathbed, sent Herndon an anecdote from 1862 when Lincoln, suffering from tooth extraction, nevertheless entertained a few visitors. He used an anecdote to illustrate the absurdity of an army plan that would follow the Yazoo River to come at the Mississippi. An analogue in Leslie's Illustrated Newspaper *(15 November 1856) told about a notable crooked tree that the hogs would crawl through twenty times a day and "every time the hogs got out they found themselves back in the same pasture again!"*

There was a man in Illinois a good many years since that was troubled with an old sow and her pigs—again and again the old man and his sons drove her out and repeatedly found her in the lot. One day he and his boys searched about and he found that she got into the lot through a certain hollow log that had been placed in the fence; they took out this log and built up the fence by placing the log a little differently than before, and the next day, what was the astonishment of the Old Lady to find that she and her litter came out of the log *outside* of the field instead of *inside*. "It is just so with the Yahoo River expedition," said Mr. L., "It comes out of the same side of the log." [59–60]

Circa 1866. Herndon interviewed Lincoln's most intimate friend, Joshua F. Speed, whose brother James served in the cabinet as attorney general. James was most likely responsible for passing the anecdote on to his brother and to mutual friend Peter Van Bergen, who also told it to Herndon. Frank B. Carpenter in Six Months at the White House *said that the boy had bought the coon with his own money. Lincoln's bodyguard William B. Crook in* Harper's Monthly *said Lincoln told the story on returning from Richmond in April 1865.[19]*

Lee had surrendered—Davis had fled, and Lincoln was joyous—Called his Cabinet together . . . and asked each one of his Cabinet what had better be done . . . Speed was sharp and hard on the Traitors—said they ought to be hung. Each one expressed their opinions—After all had expressed their opinions . . . Lincoln said I can describe my feelings by telling a story. I feel, said Lincoln—jokingly—like a little neighbor boy of mine in Indiana—his father was a hunter—he was tender and chicken hearted; his father one night caught an old coon and her young—killed the old one and all the young except one—tied a little rope around the neck of it, and told the boy to watch it while he, the father, went and got a chain—the boy was afraid his father would treat it cruelly—Lincoln went over to see the boy—the boy was apparently crying—was tender—never would throw at a bird—said to Abe—"I wish this Coon would get away—, but if I let him go, dad will whip me—, I do wish it would run off—." So I feel by these leading rebels— Davis, Lee, etc. I wish they could get away—yet if I let 'em loose—dad—the People would whip me—and yet I wish they would run away out of the land etc. [60]

Joshua Speed wrote out his recollection of a speech candidate Lincoln made in Springfield in 1836. Democrat George Forquer responded. He was a Whig turned Democrat with a lucrative office and a newly erected lightning rod on his new house. He attacked Lincoln as pretentious and too young for the legislature.

Lincoln stood near him and watched him during the whole of his speech—When Forquer concluded he took the stand again. . . . He replied to Mr. F with great dignity and force—But I shall never forget the conclusion of that speech—Turning to Mr F. he said that he had commenced his speech by announcing that this young man would have to be taken down— Turning then to the crowd he said it is for you, not for me to say whether I am up or down. The Gentleman has alluded to my being a young man—I am older in years than I am in the tricks and trades of politicians—I desire to live—and I desire place and distinction as a politician—but I would rather die now than like the gentleman live to see the day that I would have to erect a lightning rod to protect a guilty conscience from an offended God.[20]

CIRCA 1866. James Miles, Herndon's brother-in-law, reported New Salem storekeeper Samuel Hill's story about a practical joke postmaster Lincoln played on neighbor Johnson Elmore.

One Johnson—an ignorant, but ostentatious—proud man, used to go to Lincolns P.O. every day— sometimes 3 or 4 times a day—if in town, and enquire—"Anything for me"— This bored Lincoln—yet it amused him: L. fixed a plan—wrote a letter to Johnson as coming from a negress in K[entuck]y—saying many good things about opposum—dances—corn shuckings—etc. and ending—"Johns—come and see me and old master won't kick you out of my kitchen any more." Elmore took it out—opened it—couldn't read a word—pretended to read it—went and got some friends to read it—read it correctly—thought the reader was fooling him—went to others—with the same result—At last Johnson said he would get Lincoln to read it—presented it to L: it was almost too much for him—read it. The man never asked afterwards—Anything here for me.[21]

CIRCA 1866. In an interview with Herndon, James H. Matheny, a Springfield lawyer who stood up for Lincoln at his wedding, recounted his legendary putdown of Democrat E. D. Taylor during the 1840 presidential campaign and also remembered a Lincoln verse.[22]

Col. E. D. Taylor—a finely dressed—an aristocratically dressed man—having ruffle shirts—gold chain and watch etc.—was making a speech at—against the Whigs: he boasted of his Democracy [Democrats]—

called the Whigs aristocrats etc.—loomed up in his palaver—Lincoln saw it—felt devilish—thought he could take the wind out of Taylor's speech by a simple act—Lincoln nudged up—moved up to Taylor inch by inch—Lincoln raised slightly up—caught Dick Taylors vest corner— gave it a quick jerk—it unbuttoned and out fell Dick's ruffle shirt like a pile of entrails—swung out to the wind—gold chains—gold watches with large seals hung heavily and massively down. This was too much for the good People—Democrat and Whig alike—and they burst forth in a furious and uproarious laughter—Dick saw the trick—saw that it killed him—was vexed and quit and never much afterwards said even to himself *Aristocracy*.[23]

About 1837-8-9 a parcel of young men in this city formed a kind of Poetical Society—association or what not—Lincoln once or twice wrote short Poems for the book. None of the Poems are recollected in full. One verse of one, on seduction by Lincoln runs thus:

> Whatever spiteful fools may say—
> Each jealous, ranting yelper—
> No woman ever played the whore
> Unless she had a man to help her. [62]

At Herndon's repeated urging, Abner Ellis supplied several "low flung, black guard" stories—holding back the worst out of veneration for Lincoln's memory.[24] But Christopher C. Brown, another Springfield lawyer, had no such constraint. He supplied another sample of Springfield smut.

In the morning after my marriage Lincoln met me and said—"Brown why is a woman like a barrel—C.C.B. could not answer. Well, said Lincoln—You have to raise the hoops before you put the head in." [61]

From February through July 1864, from his easel in the state dining room, Frank B. Carpenter heard Lincoln's stories firsthand. Along with others compiled from the press, he printed many of them in Henry Raymond's 1865 biography. Now in his own book, Six Months at the White House, *he reprinted those and many more. The added stories given below follow Carpenter's mix of those from his own observation and those from others. Bracketed page numbers refer to his 1866 edition.*

As the different members of the Cabinet came in, the President introduced me, adding in several instances,— "He has an idea of painting a picture of us all together." This, of course, started conversation on the topic of art. Presently a reference was made by some one to [Thomas D.] Jones, the sculptor, whose bust of Mr. Lincoln was in the crimson parlor below. The President, I think, was writing at this instant. Looking up, he said, "Jones tells a good story of General [Winfield] Scott, of whom he once made a bust. Having a fine subject to start with, he succeeded in giving great satisfaction. At the closing sitting he attempted to define and elaborate the lines and markings of the face. The General sat patiently; but when he came to see the result, his countenance indicated a decided displeasure. 'Why, Jones, what have you been doing?' he asked. 'Oh,' rejoined the sculptor, 'not much, I confess, General; I have been working out the details of the face a little more, this morning.' 'Details?' exclaimed the General warmly; '—— the details! Why, my man, you are spoiling the bust!'" [34–35]

[On a walk] Something was said soon after we started about the penalty which attached to high positions in a democratic government—the tribute those filling them were compelled to pay to the public. "Great men," said Mr. Lincoln, "have various estimates. When Daniel Webster made his tour through the West years ago, he visited Springfield among other places, where great preparations had been made to receive him. As the procession was going through the town, a barefooted little darkey boy pulled the sleeve of a man named T., and asked,—'What the folks were all doing down the street?' 'Why, Jack,' was the reply, 'the biggest man in the world is coming.' Now, there lived in Springfield a man by the name of G.— a very corpulent man. Jack darted off down the street, but presently returned, with a very disappointed air. 'Well, did you see him?' inquired T. 'Yees,' returned Jack; 'but laws—he ain't half as big as old G.'" [36–37]

> *Legendary Speaker of the House of Representatives Champ Clark called a variant of Carpenter's next story "one of the finest, most effective anecdotes ever heard in Congress." He did not connect it with Lincoln. The hero of Clark's version was a "darkey" on a mule passing through a dense forest.*[25]

It was, perhaps, in connection with the newspaper attacks, that he told, during the sitting [of 2 March 1864], this story.—"A traveler on the frontier found himself out of his reckoning one night in a most inhospitable region. A terrific thunder-storm came up, to add to his trouble. He floundered along until his horse at length gave out. The lightning afforded him the only clew to his way, but the peals of thunder were frightful.

One bolt, which seemed to crash the earth beneath him, brought him to his knees. By no means a praying man, his petition was short and to the point,—'O Lord, if it is all the same to you, give us a little more light and a little less noise!'" [49]

Ward Lamon's "Administration of Lincoln" (1886) said that Lincoln told Carpenter's next anecdote in joking about an assassination: "As long as this imaginary assassin continues to exercise his amusement on others I can stand it; and I really think I am in more danger of dying from eating spinach or greens than I am from being killed by an assassin" (44). Carpenter relays it from someone attending Lincoln's meeting with a delegation of bankers.

A member of the delegation referred to the severity of the tax laid by Congress upon the State Banks. "Now," said Mr. Lincoln, "that reminds me of a circumstance that took place in a neighborhood where I lived when I was a boy. In the spring of the year the farmers were very fond of a dish which they called greens, though the fashionable name for it nowadays is spinach, I believe. One day after dinner, a large family were taken very ill. The doctor was called in, who attributed it to the greens, of which all had freely partaken. Living in the family was a half-witted boy named Jake. On a subsequent occasion, when the greens had been gathered for dinner, the head of the house said: 'Now, boys, before running any further risk in this thing, we will first try them on Jake. If he stands it, we are all right.' And just so, I suppose," said Mr. Lincoln, "Congress thought of the State Banks!" [53–54]

The source of the next anecdote was George E. Baker, who could be trusted to carry confidential documents from the State Department to the White House. He was not merely a secretary but also Secretary of State William H. Seward's longtime supporter, biographer, and editor of his Works (1884).

It was George E. Baker's province to take to the President all public documents from the State Department requiring his signature. During the first few months, Mr. Lincoln would read each paper carefully through— "I never sign a document I have not first read." As his cares increased, he departed from his habit so far as to say, "Won't you read these papers to me?" This went on for a few months, and he then modified this practice by requesting "a synopsis of its contents." His time became more and more curtailed, and for the last year his only expression was, "Show me where you want my name." [127–28]

Even White House doorkeeper Edward Moran said Lincoln told the "ugly man" story that surfaced periodically in popular literature in many guises. The London jest book Wit and Wisdom *(1826) gave it as a fact about a Mr. Lawson of the New York docks.* Harper's New Monthly Magazine *in July 1852 spoke of "a practice at the West" of giving a knife to the ugliest man and six years later said it happened to "Judge Jones of Indiana, celebrated alike for his want of beauty and his superior shrewdness as a criminal lawyer." Lincoln most likely did tell the story. Carpenter gullibly accepts it as "having actually occurred."*[26]

Mr. Lincoln was always ready to join in a laugh at the expense of his person, concerning which he was very indifferent. Many of his friends will recognize the following story,—the incident having actually occurred,—which he used to tell with great glee:—"In the days when I used to be 'on the circuit,' I was once accosted in the cars by a stranger, who said, 'Excuse me, sir, but I have an article in my possession which belongs to you.' 'How is that?' I asked, considerably astonished. The stranger took a jack-knife from his pocket. 'This knife,' said he 'was placed in my hands some years ago, with the injunction that I was to keep it until I found a man *uglier* than myself. I have carried it from that time to this. Allow me *now* to say, sir, that I think *you* are fairly entitled to the property.'" [148–49]

Swapping stories, Carpenter told Lincoln a joke about the "darkey" who prefaced his prayers by reminding the Lord that he was a good window washer. After a good laugh, Lincoln took his turn.

The story that [joke] suggests to me has no resemblance to it save in the "washing windows" part. A lady in Philadelphia had a pet poodle dog, which mysteriously disappeared. Rewards were offered for him, and a great ado made without effect. Some weeks passed, and all hope of the favorite's return had been given up, when a servant brought him in one day, in the filthiest condition imaginable. The lady was overjoyed to see her pet again, but horrified at his appearance. "Where *did* you find him!" she exclaimed. "Oh," replied the man, very unconcernedly, "a negro down the street had him tied to the end of a pole, *swabbing* windows." [159]

Carpenter missed the point of a story from General James A. Garfield telling how the president consulted veteran Flag Officer Louis Goldsborough, 8 May 1862, on plans for a joint operation to recapture Norfolk. Told that the navy had not even tried to find a landing site for the army, Lincoln and Stanton set off next day and found one themselves.[27]

Admiral, that reminds me of a chap out West who had studied law but never tried a case. Being sued, and not having confidence in his ability to manage his own case, he employed a fellow-lawyer to manage it for him. He had only a confused idea of the meaning of law terms, but was anxious to make a display of learning, and on the trial constantly made suggestions to his lawyer, who paid no attention to him. At last, fearing that his lawyer was not handling the opposing counsel very well, he lost all patience, and springing to his feet cried out, "Why don't you go at him with a *capias*, or a *surre-butter,* or something, and not stand there like a confounded old *nudum-pactum.*" [241]

Carpenter records the president adapting a popular anecdote that had appeared in Harper's Weekly, *1 June 1861, p. 339, in which the only "possibility of getting out" for the boy trapped in the cask was "through the bung-hole."*

One of Mr. Lincoln's "illustrations" in my hearing, on one occasion, was of a man who, in driving the hoops of a hogshead to "head" it up, was much annoyed by the constant falling in of the top. At length the bright idea struck him of putting his little boy inside to "hold it up." This he did; it never occurring to him till the job was done, how he was to get his child out. "This," said he, "is a fair sample of the way some people always do business." [256–57]

Carpenter gives a sanitized version of Lincoln's anecdote about a hapless schoolboy confronted with biblical names. The variant reported by Missouri senator J. B. Henderson and corroborated by Adlai Stevenson begins with Lincoln looking out the window to see three senators approaching the White House and ends with the boy exclaiming, "Look! there come them three d——d fellers again."[28]

In a time of despondency, some visitors were telling the President of the "breakers" so often seen ahead—"this time surely coming." "That," said he, "suggests the story of the school-boy, who never could pronounce the names 'Shadrach,' 'Meshach,' and 'Abednego.' He had been repeatedly whipped for it without effect. Sometime afterwards he saw the names in the regular lesson for the day. Putting his finger upon the place, he turned to his next neighbor, an older boy, and whispered, 'Here come those "tormented Hebrews" again.'" [256–57]

In the summer of 1862 Louisiana's military governor General John W. Phelps proclaimed an unauthorized emancipation. According to Carpenter (from an unnamed source), when a friend asked him why he seemed indifferent to Phelps's offense, Lincoln updated the ancient skirmish between Socrates and Xantippe .

"Well," said Mr. Lincoln, "I feel about that a good deal as a man whom I will call Jones, whom I once knew, did about his wife. He was one of your meek men, and had the reputation of being badly henpecked. At last, one day his wife was seen switching him out of the house. A day or two afterward a friend met him in the street, and said: 'Jones, I have always stood up for you, as you know; but I am not going to do it any longer. Any man who will stand quietly and take a switching from his wife, deserves to be horsewhipped.' Jones looked up with a wink, patting his friend on the back. 'Now *don't,*' said he: 'why, it didn't hurt me any; and you've no idea what a *power of good* it did Sarah Ann!'" [273–74]

From an unnamed source Carpenter relayed a description of Lincoln's anxiety about reelection in 1864.

In August 1864 prospects in the election became very gloomy. He walked two or three times across the floor in silence. "Well, I cannot run the political machine; I have enough on my hands without that. It is the people's business. If they turn their backs to the fire, and get scorched in the rear, they'll find they have got to sit on the blister!" [275]

Southern Punch for 19 March 1864 printed an anecdote about "a celebrated divine in the west country" who comes across "a little boy busily engaged in forming a miniature building of clay." To incessant questioning, the boy points out the church, the steeple, the pulpit. "Ay, but where is the minister?" "Oh, hav'na eneuch o'dirt to mak him" (9). It had nothing to do with either Lincoln or army chaplains. Carpenter cited no source in reprinting a plausible adaptation in which Lincoln is supposed to be talking to clergy seeking changes in the way chaplains were chosen. Under General Order 16 (May 1861) they were to be chosen by vote of regimental officers but after chaplains in the field complained about incompetent appointees, General Order 152 (October 1862) tightened the selection process.[29]

"Without any disrespect, gentlemen, I will tell you 'a little story.' Once, in Springfield, I was going off on a short journey, and reached the depot a little ahead of time. Leaning against the fence just outside the depot was a little darkey boy, whom I knew, named Dick, busily digging with his toe in a mud-puddle. As I came up, I said, 'Dick, what are you about?' 'Making a "church,"' said he. 'A church?' said I; 'what do you mean?' 'Why, yes,' said 'Dick,' pointing with his toe, 'don't you see? there is the shape of it; there's the "steps" and "front door"—here the "pews," where the folks set—and there's the "pulpit."' 'Yes, I see,' said I, 'but why don't you make a "minister?"' 'Laws,' answered 'Dick,' with a grin, 'I hain't got *mud* enough!'" [277]

> *The president considered predecessor John Tyler a turncoat Whig for having feuded with Lincoln's hero Henry Clay. My penultimate selection from Carpenter's* Six Months at the White House *also recalls the funeral of Tyler's predecessor the first week of April, 1841, when the elaborate ceremonies concluded at "a funeral car specially constructed for the occasion."[30]*

One of the last stories I heard from Mr. Lincoln was concerning John Tyler, for whom it was to be expected, as an old Henry Clay Whig, he would entertain no great respect. "A year or two after Tyler's accession to the Presidency," said he, "contemplating an excursion in some direction, his son went to order a special train of cars. It so happened that the railroad superintendent was a very strong Whig. On 'Bob's' making known his errand, that official bluntly informed him that his road did not run any special trains for the President. 'What!' said 'Bob,' did you not furnish a special train for the funeral of General Harrison?' 'Yes,' said the superintendent, stroking his whiskers, 'and if you will only bring your father here in that shape, you shall have the best train on the road.'" [278]

> *In recounting Lincoln's "last story," Carpenter confused facts about the fateful evening of 14 April 1865. After supper, Speaker Colfax discussed reconvening the Confederate legislature. After that discussion, ex-congressman George Ashmun came in to schedule an interview for the next day. Worst for Carpenter's memory, Provost Marshal Ward Lamon was out of town on a mission to Richmond. It could have happened on some earlier date, but the story would have suffered loss of sentimental appeal.*

The last story told by Mr. Lincoln was drawn out by a circumstance which occurred just before the interview with Messrs. Colfax and Ashmun, on the evening of his assassination. Marshal Lamon of Washington had called upon him with an application for the pardon of a soldier. After a brief hearing the President took the application, and when about to write his name upon the back of it, he looked up and said: "Lamon, have you ever heard how the Patagonians eat oysters? They open them and throw the shells out the window until the pile gets higher than the house, and then they move;" adding: "I feel to-day like commencing a new pile of pardons, and I may as well begin it just here." [284–85]

1867

OCTOBER. Even after Six Months at the White House *went through several editions, Carpenter kept contributing stories to the press. In an unidentified newspaper clipping after 28 September 1867, he told about Lincoln's remark to a delegation of bankers brought to his office by Comptroller of Currency Hugh McCulloch.*

Mr. Lincoln was writing at his desk by the window of his office as the party entered. Mr. McCulloch went to him, and, leaning over the desk, said: "Mr. President, I wish to introduce to you a number of financial gentlemen who have come to Washington to see about the new loan. As bankers, they are obliged to hold our national securities, and I can therefore vouch for their loyalty; for you know how the good book says, "Where the treasure is, there will the *heart* be also!" Mr. Lincoln, without looking up, instantly replied, "There is another version of that, Mr. McCulloch. The same book says 'Where the *carcass* is there will the *eagles* be gathered together.'"

1869

31 MARCH. Rev. Abraham Goodpasture, of the Sangamon Presbytery since before 1850, complied with William Herndon's request for anecdotes. Infected by Carpenter or not, he sent an affidavit about a similar exchange of biblical quips.

About the A.D. 1846 Mr. Lincoln visited Petersburg and as usual quite a number of citizens gathered near to him; evinceing great pleasure in hearing him talk, and every now and then he would tell some joke causing all to manifest pleasure in his society: after some time in his company I passed on giving attention to the business of the day, and after an hour or so I returned back along the street, and still there was quite a croud with Mr. Lincoln, all in good glee, and as I was passing them, I thought I would say something, and remarked that Where the great ones are there will the people be. Mr. Lincoln replyed Ho! *Parson* a little more Scriptural: "Where the carces is there will the eagels be gathered togather:" There was quite a laugh, and so I passed on. I know this to be truth.[31]

In Recollections of Men and Things at Washington, *Lawrence Gobright, an Associated Press Washington correspondent for many years, recalled the president's response when two congressmen brought five six-footers to meet him.*

After carefully surveying the tall specimens, the President exclaimed, "Are they all from your State?" "All," was the spontaneous response. "Why, it seems to me," said the President, glancing at the short Representatives, "that your State always sends *little* men to Congress." [329]

1878

FEBRUARY–MARCH. Noah Brooks, editor and correspondent for the Sacramento Union *(where he edited Mark Twain's* Innocents Abroad*) and a friend of Lincoln's for a decade, would have become the president's secretary; instead, he became his biographer, beginning with the series "Personal Reminiscences of Lincoln" in* Scribner's Monthly Magazine.*[32] His first anecdote recounts Lincoln's affectionate retelling of a scene from one of his favorite comic authors, "Orpheus C. Kerr" (R. H. Newell), in which a member of the Pennsylvania Mud-larks is about to have his leg amputated and pleads for his grandmother.*[33]

The point in the story was that a messenger was sent to the navy department to implore Secretary Welles to personate the grandmother for this occasion only, and that he declined with regret, giving as his excuse that he was very busy examining a model of Noah's ark, with a view to its introduction into the United States Navy. Having told this anecdote, Lincoln turned to me and said, "I hope Mr. Welles will never hear that I told this story on him." Somewhat nettled by his manner, I said, good-humoredly, "It will not be your fault, Mr. President, if he does not hear of it, for I have heard you tell it at least a dozen times." [78]

Lincoln particularly liked a joke at the expense of the dignity of some high civil or military official. One day, not long before his second inauguration, he asked me if I had heard about Stanton's meeting a picket on Broad River, South Carolina, and then told this story: "Gen. [J. G.] Foster, then at Port Royal, escorted the secretary up the river, taking a quartermaster's tug. Reaching the outer lines on the river, a picket roared from the bank, 'Who have you got on board that tug?' The severe and dignified answer was, 'The secretary of war and Major-General Foster.' Instantly the picket roared back, 'We've got major-generals enough up here— why don't you bring us up some hard-tack?'" [78–79]

> *The next anecdote from Noah Brooks's "Personal Reminiscences" had an analogue in the seventeenth century: the soldier losing his mug cries out, "Zounds! the drink's all spilt." In 1866 the mug had changed into a cartridge. The soldier who has it shot out of his hand cooly faced "the direction from which the shot came . . ." and exclaimed: "You can't do that again, old fellow."[34]*

And there was another one of a soldier at the battle of Chancellorsville, whose regiment, waiting to be called into the fight, was taking coffee. The hero of the story put to his lips a crockery mug which he had carried, with infinite care, through several campaigns. A stray bullet, just missing the coffee-drinker's head, dashed the mug into fragments and left only its handle on his finger. Turning his head in that direction, the soldier angrily growled, "Johnny, you can't do that again!" [79]

> *One of Brooks's more charming reminiscences is of the jovial intimacy between twelve-year-old Tad Lincoln and his father on the day of his reelection while he and Brooks were discussing returns.*

Lincoln was as bright and cheery as the beautiful November day. He had a new story of Tad's wit and humor; for the lad was very clever. Tad had burst into his father's office, early in the day, with the information that the detachment of Pennsylvania troops, quartered on the White House grounds, on the Potomac front, "were voting for Lincoln and Johnson." The excited lad insisted on his father's going to the window to see this spectacle. Seeing a pet turkey which had been spared from the cook's knife, at Christmas, in answer to Tad's tearful petition, Lincoln said, "What business had the turkey stalking about the polls in that way? Does he vote?" "No," was the quick reply of the boy, "he's not of age." [79–80]

> *Showing Lincoln's knack for giving a good story "peculiar crispness and freshness," Brooks told about Lincoln reading a newspaper account of a captain accused of embezzling company funds who took that charge lightly but when a new charge of disloyalty was added became enraged. Lincoln was reminded of a story. Brooks was unsure whether it was of his own experience or secondhand.*

This fellow reminds me of a juror in a case of hen stealing which I tried in Illinois, many years ago. The accused man was summarily convicted. After adjournment of court, as I was riding to the next town, one of the jurors in the case came cantering up behind me and complimented me on the vigor with which I had pressed the prosecution of the unfortunate hen-thief. Then he added, "Why, when I was young, and my back was strong, and the country was new, I didn't mind taking off a sheep now and then. But stealing hens! Oh, Jerusalem!" Now, this captain has evidently been stealing sheep, and that is as much as he can bear. [80]

CIRCA CHRISTMASTIME. George Alfred Townsend, Washington columnist for the Chicago Tribune *and* Cincinnati Enquirer, *kept a scrapbook in which he entered an anecdote from Lincoln's secretary of interior, John Palmer Usher, that would not have been fit for his column.*

Said Mr. Usher: When I met Lincoln at Paris Illinois somewhere about 1844 it was told me that he had a lot of new stories which I ought to hear; and we were gathered together at the Hotel to hear him put them out. One story I remember distinctly. It was about a person who had a great veneration for Revolutionary relics. He heard that an old lady in a certain portion of Illinois had a dress which she had worn in the Revolutionary War. He made a special visit to this lady and asked her if she could produce the dress as a satisfaction to his love of aged things. She obliged him by opening a drawer and bringing out the article in question. The enthusiastic person took up the dress and delivered an apostrophe to it. "Were you the dress," said he, "that this lady once young and blooming wore in the time of Washington? No doubt when you came home from the dressmaker she kissed you as I do now!" At this the relic hunter took the old dress and kissed it heartily. The practical old lady rather resented such foolishness over an old piece of wearing apparel and she said: "Stranger if you want to kiss something old you had better kiss my ass. It is sixteen years older than that dress."[35]

OCTOBER. In Scribner's Monthly *General Egbert Viele, once military governor of Norfolk, recalled visiting Fort Monroe in 1862 with Lincoln and secretaries Salmon P. Chase and Edwin M. Stanton. Stanton explained how he had received an urgent telegram asking instructions that he did not understand and answered in haste, "All right; go ahead," and then told the president.*

"I suppose you meant," said Mr. Lincoln, "that it was all right if it was good for him, and all wrong if it was not. That reminds me," said he, "of a story about a horse that was sold at the cross-roads near where I once lived. The horse was supposed to be fast, and quite a number of people were present at the time appointed for the sale. A small boy was employed to ride the horse backward and forward to exhibit his points. One of the would-be buyers followed the boy down the road and asked him confidentially if the horse had a splint. 'Well, mister,' said the boy, 'if it's good for him he has got it, but if it isn't good for him he hasn't.'"[36]

Viele also recalled how on that same trip Lincoln talked about a weakness of his own.

If I have one vice, and I can call it nothing else, it is not to be able to say no! Thank God for not making me a woman, but if He had, I suppose He would have made me just as ugly as He did, and no one would ever have tempted me. It was only the other day, a poor parson whom I knew some years ago in Joliet came to the White House with a sad story of his poverty and his large family—poor parsons seem always to have large families—and he wanted me to do something for him. I knew very well that I could do nothing for him, and yet I couldn't bear to tell him so, and so I said I would see what I could do. The very next day the man came back for the office which he said that I had promised him—which was not true, but he seemed really to believe it. Of course there was nothing left for me to do except to get him a place through one of the secretaries. But if I had done my duty, I should have said "no" in the beginning.[37]

1881

16 JUNE. Among earliest of reliable Lincoln biographers and an influential political ally in Congress, Isaac N. Arnold spoke in London to the Royal Historical Society. He retailored an old Irish bull, as in The American Jest Book *(1833), where the Irish immigrant insists that his family has voted against the government, "since the time of the flood" (14). Arnold imitated Lincoln using dialect as he responds to a good-humored British official's tease in 1864: "I understand, Mr. President, everybody votes in this country. If we remain until November can we vote?"*

"You remind me," replied the President, "of a countryman of yours, a green emigrant from Ireland. Pat arrived in New York on election day, and was, perhaps, as eager as Your Excellency to vote, and to vote early and late and often. So, upon his landing at Castle Garden, he hastened to the nearest voting place, and, as he approached, the judge, who received the ballots, inquired, 'who do you want to vote for? On which side are you?' Poor Pat was embarrassed, he did not know who were the candidates. He stopped, scratched his head, then, with the readiness of his countrymen, he said: 'I am fornent the Government, anyhow. Tell me, if your Honor plases, which is the rebellion side, and I'll tell you how I want to vote. In Ould Ireland, I was always on the rebellion side, and, by Saint Patrick, I'll stick to that same in America.'"[38]

1882

Indefatigable collector Osborne H. I. Oldroyd knew Lincoln only in print but collected books, correspondence, and ephemera now part of Ford's Theater Museum and sampled in Oldroyd's Lincoln Memorial: Album Immortelles *(1882), source of the next extracts. The first is from Rev. George Minier, who had known Lincoln as a lawyer on the Eighth Judicial Circuit; the second is from Glenni W. Scofield, an early Republican from Pennsylvania and six-term congressman. Minier remembered how Lincoln addressed the tariff using a sketch common in seventeenth-century popular literature, most recently adapted in Seba Smith's "My First Visit to Portland," as reprinted in W. S. Burton's* Cyclopedia of Wit and Humor *(1858). Chicago lawyer John J. McGilvra said Lincoln told the same story in different circumstances.[39]*

There is something obscure about [the tariff]. It reminds me of the fellow that came into a grocery store down here in Menard County, at Salem, where I once lived, and called for a picayune's worth of crackers; so the clerk laid them out on the counter. After sitting awhile, he said to the clerk, "I don't want these crackers, take them, and give me a glass of cider." So the clerk put the crackers back in the box, and handed the fellow the cider. After drinking, he started for the door. "Here, Bill," called out the clerk, "pay me for your cider." "Why," said Bill, "I gave you the crackers for it." "Well, then, pay me for the crackers." "But I hain't had any," responded Bill. "That's so," said the clerk. "Well, clear out! It seems to me that I've lost a picayune somehow, but I can't make it out exactly." "So," said Lincoln, after the laugh had subsided, "it is with the tariff; somebody gets the picayune, but I don't exactly understand how."

Congressman Scofield sought a pardon for a soldier convicted of knocking down his captain. Lincoln told him to let Congress handle it.

I inquired what Congress could do in the matter, and quick as thought he said: "Pass a law that a private shall have a right to knock down his captain." But after the wit came the pardon.

1883

Thurlow Weed's autobiography provided anecdotes recollected by this veteran Republican, Albany editor, and New York state powerbroker to whom the president routinely turned for political advice and assistance. In the first of two extracts, Lincoln has been discussing a politician from Maryland.

"Maryland must, I think, be like New Hampshire, a good State to move from." And then he told a story of a witness in a neighboring county, who, on being asked his age, replied, "Sixty." Being satisfied that he was much older, the judge repeated the question, and on receiving the same answer, admonished the witness, saying that the court knew him to be much older than sixty. "Oh," said the witness, "you're thinking about that fifteen year that I lived down on the eastern shore of Maryland; that was so much lost time and don't count."

During a convivial conversation, Weed quips that his appetite for sausage depends on whether pork was cheaper than dogs. That triggered Lincoln's tale of prairie vengeance.

"That," said Mr. Lincoln, "reminds me of what occurred down at Joliet, where a popular grocer supplied all the villagers with sausages. One Saturday evening, when his grocery was filled with customers, for whom he and his boys were busily engaged in weighing sausages, a neighbor with whom he had had a violent quarrel that day came into the grocery, made his way up to the counter, holding two enormous dead cats by the tail, which he deliberately threw on the counter, saying, 'This makes seven to-day. I'll call round on Monday and get my money for them.'"[40]

1884

Reminiscences of Abraham Lincoln *by his intimate friend Joshua Fry Speed reported Lincoln telling a story in 1862 that had also appeared in the popular newspaper* Spirit of the Times *five years earlier. When a delegation complained about military affairs in the West, the president replied with an anecdote he says he had heard at Burlington, Iowa.*

He was trying to enforce upon his hearers the truth of the old adage that three moves is worse than a fire. As an illustration he gave an account of a family who started from Western Pennsylvania, pretty well off in this world's goods when they started. But they moved and moved, having less and less every time they moved, till after a while they could carry every thing in one wagon. He said that the chickens of the family got so used to being moved, that whenever they saw the wagon sheets brought out they laid themselves on their backs and crossed their legs, ready to be tied. "Now, gentlemen, if I were to listen to every committee that comes in at that door, I had just as well cross my hands and let you tie me."[41]

Speed included Lincoln's adaptation of an Aesop fable in replying to a suggestion from William Cabell Rives, an Old Whig U.S. senator from Virginia, when Lincoln was in Congress. In 1861 he served on a Washington commission seeking to avoid the war. Speed's story supposes that Rives advised surrendering Federal forts and property in southern states. The end of Lincoln's fable differs from the contemporary translation of Aesop by Thomas James in which the woodsman merely drives away "the unreasonable suitor."[42]

Mr. Lincoln asked him if he remembered the fable of the Lion and the Woodsman's Daughter. Mr. Reeves said that he did not. "Aesop," said the President, "reports that a lion was very much in love with a woodsman's daughter. The fair maid, afraid to say no, referred him to her father. The lion applied for the girl. The father replied, your teeth are too long. The lion went to a dentist and had them extracted. Returning, he asked for his bride. No, said the woodsman, your claws are too long. Going back to the dentist, he had them drawn. Then, returning to claim his bride, the woodsman, seeing that he was disarmed, beat out his brains. May it not be so," said Mr. Lincoln, "with me, if I give up all that is asked."[43]

1885

After a distinguished naval career during the war, Admiral David D. Porter turned to history and fiction—a combination that could have shaded his memory of the three anecdotes sampled here from his Incidents and Anecdotes of the Civil War. *The first reports*

Lincoln's comment when Secretary of State Seward interfered with naval operations.

This looks to me very much like the case of two fellows I once knew; one was a gambler, the other a preacher. They met in a stage, and the gambler induced the preacher to play poker, and the latter won all the gambler's money. "It's all because we have mistaken our trades," said the gambler; "you ought to have been a gambler and I a preacher, and, by ginger, I intend to turn the tables on you next Sunday and preach in your church," which he did.

Porter tells of going with Secretary of the Navy Gideon Welles to propose a plan to capture New Orleans. Wishing more aggressive planning, the president applied a down-home story.

There was an old woman in Illinois who missed some of her chickens and couldn't imagine what had become of them. Someone suggested that they had been carried off by a skunk; so she told her husband he must sit up that night and shoot the critter. The old man sat up all night and next morning came in with two pet rabbits. "Thar," he said, "your chickens are all safe; thar's two of them skunks I killed." "Them ain't skunks," said the old woman, "them's my pet rabbits; you allers was a fool!" "Well, then," returned the old man, "if them ain't skunks I don't know a skunk when I sees it." Now, Mr. Secretary, the navy has been hunting pet rabbits long enough; suppose you send them after skunks.

When the president sailed to Richmond, Porter's ship was so large that the party transferred to a barge. Lincoln commented with a story commonly ascribed to Andrew Jackson, as in Francis Grund's Aristocracy in America *(1839), 250–51, and more recently in the* Southern Review *(April 1873): 372.*

Admiral, this brings to my mind a fellow who once came to me to ask for an appointment as minister abroad. Finally, he asked to be made a tidewaiter. When he saw he could not get that, he asked me for an old pair of trousers. But it is well to be humble.[44]

1886

Editor of the cosmopolitan New York monthly North American Review, *Allen Thorndike Rice seems to have scoured the land for eyewitness contributors to his popular volume of* Reminiscences of Abraham Lincoln by Distinguished Men of His Time. *The book quickly grew from 428 pages and twenty essays to 650 pages and thirty-three essays. Writers ranged from intimates like U. S. Grant to observers like Walt Whitman, aiming at immediacy rather than posterity. Page references following the extracts refer to Rice's first edition.*

U. S. Grant's son Frederic submitted anecdotes deleted from his father's just-published autobiography. The first said that in March 1864, shortly after promoting U. S. Grant to lieutenant general, the president had told him a fable by Orpheus C. Kerr from The Palace Beautiful and Other Poems *(1865), 130–40. That poem was about Jocko the monkey, who thought he could be a great general if only he had a longer tail. Gideon Welles's diary for 17 June 1863 said Lincoln used the poem to illustrate McClellan's call for more troops. Both David D. Porter and Horace Porter corroborate Lincoln's repeating the black-smith anecdote—varying a Davy Crockett story—in spring 1864.*[45]

So they got more tail and spliced it on to his caudal appendage. He looked at it admiringly, and then thought he ought to have a little more still. This was added, and again he called for more. The splicing process was repeated many times, until they had coiled Jocko's tail around the room, filling all the space. Still he called for more tail, and, there being no other place to coil it, they began wrapping it around his shoulders. He continued his call for more, and they kept on winding the additional tail about him until its weight broke him down. [1–2]

Upon one occasion, when the President was at my head-quarters at City Point [22 June 1864] I took him to see the work that had been done on the Dutch Gap Canal. After taking him around and showing him all the points of interest, explaining how, in blowing up one portion of the work that was being excavated, the explosion had thrown the material back into, and filled up, a part already completed, he turned to me and said: "Grant, do you know what this reminds me of? Out in Springfield, Illinois, there was a blacksmith named ____. One day, when he did not have much to do, he took a piece of soft iron that had been in his shop for some time, and for which he had no special use, and, starting up his fire, began to heat it. When he got it hot he carried it to the anvil and began to hammer it, rather thinking he would weld it into an agricultural implement. He pounded away for some time until he got it fashioned into some shape, when he discovered that the iron would not hold out to complete the implement he had in mind. He then put it back into the forge, heated it up again, and recommenced hammering, with an ill-defined notion that he would make a claw-hammer. Again he heated it, and thought he would make an axe. After hammering and welding it into shape, knocking the oxydized iron off in flakes, he concluded there was not enough of the iron left to make an axe that would be of any use. He was now getting tired and a little disgusted at the result of his various essays. So he filled his forge full of coal, and, after placing the iron in the center of the heap, took the bellows and worked up a tremendous blast, bringing the iron to a white heat. Then with his tongs he lifted it from the bed of coals, and thrusting it into a tub of water near by, exclaimed with an oath, "Well, if I can't make anything else of you, I will make a fizzle, anyhow." [2–4]

> *George W. Julian, a Whig congressman from Indiana, a founder of the Republican Party, and a passionate promoter of abolition, submitted a sampling of Lincoln jokes and puns to Rice's collection. The first is prompted by the problem of what to do with General J. C. Fremont, the second is in answer to a warning that giving Fremont a command would stir up trouble, the third is in respect to the Emancipation Proclamation. The third had appeared in* Old Abe's Joker *(1863), 54, about a dog and in the* Proceedings of the Worcester Society of Antiquities *(1879), 42, about a sheep.*

He did not know where to place him, and . . . it reminded him of the old man who advised his son to take a wife, to which the young man responded, "Whose wife shall I take?" [55]

[Reassigning Fremont] would stir the country favorably on one side and stir it the other way on the other. It would please Fremont's friends and displease the conservatives; and that is all I can see in the stirring argument. [55]

He likened the case to that of the boy, who, when asked how many legs his calf would have if he called the tail a leg, replied, "Five"; to which the prompt response was, "Calling the tail a leg would not make it a leg." [62]

> *Reuben E. Fenton, former Republican congressman and governor of New York, recalled the president's consternation over General McClellan's inertia in December 1861.*

Providence, with favoring sky and earth, seemed to beckon the army on, but General McClellan, he supposed, knew his business and had his reasons for disregarding these hints of Providence. And as we have got to stand by the General . . . I think a good way to do it may be for Congress to take a recess for several weeks, and by the time you get together again, if McClellan is not off with the army, Providence is very likely to step in with hard roads and force us to say, "the army can't move." You know Dickens said of a certain man that if he would always follow his nose he would never stick fast in the mud. Well, when the rains set in it will be impossible for even our eager and gallant soldiers to keep their noses so high that their feet will not stick in the clay mud of Old Virginia. [74–75]

*Benjamin Perley Poore, longtime Washington insider, correspondent for Boston newspapers, and clerk of the Senate's printing records, submitted a still popular story about Lincoln in the Black Hawk war that in his own day starred "a country captain" (*Leslie's Illustrated Newspaper, *26 May 1860) or "a Volunteer Rifle captain" (*Harper's Weekly, *28 July 1860), but not Lincoln.*

I remember his narrating his first experience in drilling his company. He was marching with a front of over twenty men across a field, when he desired to pass through a gateway into the next inclosure. "I could not for the life of me," said he, "remember the proper word of command for getting my company endwise so that it could get through the gate, so as we came near the gate I shouted: 'This company is dismissed for two minutes, when it will fall in again on the other side of the gate!'" [88]

A more reliable contributor to Rice's collection, Titian J. Coffey served as Lincoln's assistant attorney general. He reported to the president that U.S. marshals wanted their own legal defense fund. A delegation came seeking a favor.

"Yes," said he, "[the marshals] will now all be after the money and be content with nothing else. They are like the man in Illinois whose cabin was burned down, and according to the kindly custom of early days in the West, his neighbors all contributed something to start him again. In his case they had been so liberal that he soon found himself better off than before the fire, and he got proud. One day, a neighbor brought him a bag of oats, but the fellow refused it with scorn. 'No,' said he, 'I'm not taking oats now. I take nothing but money.'" [88]

A friend of mine was one of a delegation who called on Mr. Lincoln to ask the appointment of a gentleman as Commissioner to the Sandwich Islands. They presented their case as earnestly as possible, and, besides his fitness for the place, they urged that he was in bad health, and a residence in that balmy climate would be of great benefit to him. the President closed the interview with this discouraging remark: "Gentlemen, I am sorry to say that there are eight other applicants for that place, and they are all sicker than your man." [88–89]

Schuyler Colfax recalled how on 13 September 1862 Lincoln issued his reasoned response to the delegation from Chicago presenting popular petitions for emancipation.[46] *Colfax added the story that one of the preachers insisted "it is a message to you from our Divine Master, through me, commanding you, sir, to open the doors of bondage."*

Mr. Lincoln replied instantly. "That may be, sir . . . but is it not odd that the only channel he could send it by was that roundabout route by that awfully wicked city of Chicago?" [335]

James B. Fry, an artillery officer who rose to become provost marshal general and had been assigned to escort the president to the Gettysburg commemoration, remembered Lincoln telling this popular favorite. Variations had appeared in the London jest book Court Jester, *published circa 1790, and Hans Andersen's "Tinder Box."*[47]

At the appointed time I went to the White House, where I found the President's carriage at the door to take him to the station; but he was not ready. When he appeared it was rather late, and I remarked that he had no time to lose in going to the train. "Well," said he, "I feel about that as the convict in one of our Illinois towns felt when he was going to the gallows. As he passed along the road in custody of the sheriff, the people, eager to see the execution, kept crowding and pushing past him. At last he called out: 'Boys, you needn't be in such a hurry to get ahead, *there won't be any fun till I get there.*'" [89]

Ohioan David Ross Locke, as "Petroleum V. Nasby," popular comic columnist, authored the satirical sketches that Lincoln enjoyed reading hours before being assassinated. Locke interviewed Lincoln before he became president.

In an interview [about 1858] the name came up of a recently deceased politician of Illinois, whose undeniable merit was blemished by an overweening vanity. His funeral was very largely attended: "If General —— had known how big a funeral he would have had," said Mr. Lincoln, "he would have died years ago." [90]

In September 1859, Locke asked his opinion of Illinois outlawing interracial marriage and of Republican interparty squabbling.

The law means nothing. I shall never marry a negress, but I have no objection to anyone else doing so. If a white man wants to marry a negro woman, let him do it—if the negro woman can stand it. [446–47]

I learned a great many years ago, that in a fight between man and wife, a third party should never get between the woman's skillet and the man's axe-helve. [451]

Donn Piatt, another Ohio journalist and also a wartime colonel, recollected Lincoln's comment back in Springfield about threats of secession.

They won't give up the [public] offices. Were it believed that vacant places could be had at the North Pole, the road would be lined with dead Virginians. [481]

Edward W. Andrews, an assistant adjutant general, accompanied the president to Gettysburg in place of a general inflicted with boils. This triggered Lincoln's story about such an affliction.

Not long ago, when Colonel ——, with his cavalry, was at the front, and the Rebs were making things rather lively for us, the colonel was ordered out on a *reconnaisance.* He was troubled at the time with a big boil where it made horseback riding decidedly uncomfortable. He hadn't gone more than two or three miles when he declared he couldn't stand it any longer, and dismounted and ordered his troops forward without him. He had just settled down to enjoy his relief from change of position when he was startled by the rapid reports of pistols and the helter-skelter approach of his troops in full retreat before a yelling rebel force. He forgot everything but the yells, sprang into his saddle, and made capital time over fences and ditches till safe within the lines. The pain from his boil was gone, and the boil too, and the colonel swore that there was no cure for boils so sure as fright from rebel yells, and that the secession had rendered to loyalty *one* valuable service at any rate. [90]

Ward Hill Lamon had ridden the Eighth Judicial Circuit with Lincoln and considered himself the president's personal bodyguard, and yet his memoirs of the administration plus the files of notes compiled by his daughter seem based on reading rather than on observation. The

extract from his draft of "Administration of Lincoln" (1886) could
have been adapted by Lincoln from his old favorite, Artemus Ward's "A
Sad Case," in which a fourteen-year-old Arkansas lad pleads: "I hope
your Honor will show some consideration for the feelings of a poor
orphan."[48] Lamon's version has a lady demanding that a hospital be
reconverted to its original use as a church.

Afterwards in speaking of this incident Mr. Lincoln said that the lady as
a representative of her class in Alexandria reminded him of the story of
the young man who had an aged father and mother owning considerable
property. The young man being an only son and believing that the old
people had lived out their usefulness assassinated them both. He was
accused, tried and convicted. When the judge came to pass sentence
upon him and called upon him to give any reason he might have why the
sentence of death should not be passed upon him, he with great prompt-
ness replied he hoped the court would be lenient with him because he
was a poor orphan.[49]

1887

General George B. McClellan's memoirs said Lincoln told a story after
a telegram from the field reported few casualties in proportion to the
fierceness of the battle. An analogue in The Family Joe Miller *(1848)*
has a friend rather than a servant who interrupts. The friend says,
"Zounds, if you had not trod upon my toe, I should have made it as
broad as it was long" (91).

 The President quietly listened to my reading of the telegram, and then
said it reminded him of a notorious liar, who attained such a reputation as
an exaggerator that he finally instructed his servant to stop him when his
tongue was running too rapidly, by pulling his coat or touching his feet.
One day the master was relating wonders he had seen in Europe, and
described a building which was about a mile long and a half-mile high.
Just then the servant's heel came down on the narrator's toes, and he
stopped abruptly. One of the listeners asked how broad this remarkable
building might be; the narrator replied, "About a foot!"[50]

Seventy-eight-year-old William Herndon and another Lincoln enthusi-
ast, Hoosier Jesse Weik, forty-one, collaborated on Herndon's Lincoln:
The True Story of a Great Life, *incorporating the letters and inter-*
views of twenty-five years along with additional material that Weik

collected himself and squeezed from Herndon's aging memory. Their papers, now at the Library of Congress, were published as Herndon's Informants *in a magnificent edition by my old friends Rodney Davis and Douglas Wilson for the University of Illinois Press in 1998. My text is from the Library of Congress manuscripts, but page references in brackets refer to Davis and Wilson's edition.*

[*Henry C. Whitney remembered Lincoln bedeviled by office-seekers:*] I was in Washington in the Indian service for a few days before August and I merely said to Lincoln one day—"Everything is drifting into the war and I guess you will have to put me in the army." He said "I'm making Generals now and in a few days I will be making Quartermasters and then I'll fix you." [619]

[*Whitney also recounted incidents during their circuit-riding days.*] He was at Urbana once prosecuting a man named A.G. Carle in Urbana for seduction and one S.H. Busey an adverse witness tried to create the impression that he was a great ladies man. Lincoln went for him in his speech thus, "There's Busey—he pretends to be a great heart smasher—does wonderful things with the girls—but I'll venture that he never entered his flesh but once and that is when he fell down and stuck his finger in his ——" right out in open Court. Things were free and easy in Urbana and Danville. [630]

Herndon's repeated prodding produced more anecdotes from Henry C. Whitney. This one had been circulating as far back as Pascal's Provincial Letters *(14 December 1656) and more recently in* The Humorist's Own Book *(1834), where it was told about William III complaining about Archbishop Tillotson's long sermons.*

The first story I ever heard Lincoln tell was in court. Court stopped to hear—"Its like the lazy preacher who used to read very long sermons: when asked how so lazy a man used to write such long sermons, one of the deacons said, 'Oh! he gets to writing and is too lazy to stop.'" [643]

Sonora, Kentucky, postmaster Charles Friend wrote to Herndon about Dr. Jesse H. Rodman's visiting the White House, where he presented the president with a gold-headed cane. Lincoln alluded to a popular Irish bull. It had appeared in The Percy Anecdotes *(1852) and more recently in* Harper's Weekly, *18 February 1865. He next asked about friends of his childhood, especially playmate Austin Golliher.*

Lincoln sayed how will I know who gave [the cane] to me, Dr says the names of the Donars will be ingraved on it "to the President A Lincoln," Abe sayed what a fool, I am like the Irishman that went to the Post Office and when the Post Master asked his name sayed "faith, an't my name on the lether" of course my name will be on the cane. [676]

Sayed Abe "I would rather see Golliher than any man living, he played me a dirty trick once and I want to pay him up, One Sunday Golliher and another boy and my self wer out in the woods on knob Creek playing and hunting around for young squirrels when I climbed up a tree and left Austin and the other boy on the grown shortly Golliher shut his eyes like he was a sleep I noticed his hat sat straight with the reverse side up I thought I would shit in his hat Golliher was watching and when I let the load drop he swapd hats and my hat caught the whole charge," At this recital the President laughed heartily. [676]

In turn, Weik prodded Herndon to unlock the horde of anecdotes entombed in memories of more than forty years with Lincoln dead and alive. When the term "locofoco" puzzled young Weik, Herndon told him to look it up. Lincoln thought them frauds for claiming direct descent from the Founding Fathers. His illustration, as Herndon remembered it, was about the farmer who one night hears a racket in the hen house.

On going into the hen house he looked around on the floor and in the roosts and at last found his enemy, a pole cat crouched in the corner with two or three dead chickens. The farmer seized the pole cat and dragged him out and all who know the nature of such a cat know what followed—a devil of a stink. The pole cat demurred as well as he could in his own language saying that he was no such brute as charged, but an innocent animal and a friend of the farmer just come to take care of his chickens. The farmer to this replied—"You look like a pole cat—just the size of a pole cat—act like one," snuffin up his nose "and smell like one and you are one by God, and I'll kill you, innocent and as friendly to me as you say you are." "These locofocos," said Lincoln "claim to be true democrats, but they are only locofocos—they look like locofocos—just the size of locofocos—act like locofocos—and" turning up his nose and backing away a little on the Stand as if the smell was about to smother him "are locofocos by God."[51]

Herndon sent Weik a six-page "Law Story" that he said Lincoln laughed over—"That case beat me, badly—more than any I ever had." About

77

1850 in Coles County the court assigned him to defend a hog stealer who was clearly guilty yet refused to confide in Lincoln, assuring him that they would win the verdict—as they did. Lincoln in all innocence took him aside to learn the secret of their success.

The man at last said—"Well Lincoln my good fellow I'll tell you. I did steal the hogs and more of 'em than I was indicted for—many more and sold 'em to my neighbors, the jury: They knew that if I was convicted that they would have to pay for the hogs that I sold 'em, as they belonged to Mr — and Mr —— and the jury knew it from the evidence. Now Lincoln do you see where the joke is?" . . . Lincoln was astonished at the fellow and his story: he used to tell the story on circuit with great gusto and to the delight of his brother attorneys of the bar.[52]

. As an example of a story Lincoln "loved to tell," Herndon sent Weik the one about a man of whom Lincoln said, "I worshipped the fellow." Herndon added an uncharacteristic disclaimer: "As a matter of course no such thing ever happened and yet it is a good story to show the power of audacity." The scene has ladies and gentlemen at "a fine table."

After the men and women had enjoyed themselves by dancing—promenading—flirting etc they were told that the supper was set. The man of audacity—quick witted—self possessed and equal to all occasions was put at the head of the table to carve the turkeys, chickens and pigs. The men and women surrounded the table and the audacious man being chosen carver whetted his great carving knife with the steel and got down to business and commenced carving the turkey, but he expended too much force and let a fart— a loud fart so that all the people heard it distinctly. . . . A deep silence reigned. However the audacious man was cool and entirely self possessed; he was curiously and keenly watched by those who knew him well, they suspecting that he would recover in the end and acquit himself with glory. The man with a kind of sublime audacity, pulled off his coat, rolled up his sleeves—put his coat deliberately on a chair—spat on his hands—took his position at the head of the table— picked up the carving knife and whetted it again, never cracking a smile nor moving a muscle of his face. It now became a wonder in the minds of all the men and women how the fellow was to get out of his dilemma; he squared himself and said loudly and distinctly—"Now by God I'll see if I can't cut up this turkey without farting."[53]

With the next story sent to Weik, Herndon added a devastating note. He said that Lincoln had told the story in 1862–63 to "Judge

[Lawrence] Weldon and others who told it to me and I at the time wrote it out and put it in a small book which I loaned to [Ward] Lamon, but can't get it back." That book is still missing, along with similar notebooks Lincoln must have carried for such occasions. Meanwhile, Herndon tells of a mother in southern Illinois who doted on one of her boys, aged twelve or fourteen, and would praise him and have him say and do smart things when company came.

The boy one day got sleepy and so he thought he would retire and go to sleep in the trundle bed which rolled under the larger bed and out again as circumstances required. The boy crawled into bed and at the same time a large she cat—a pet—one of the house, went to bed with him. Soon after the boy went to bed some ladies and gentlemen called in to see the family. As was the custom and habit of the mother lady, she commenced eulogizing her fine, pretty and moral boy and at last to clinch the argument and to have the boy exhibit himself in proof of what she said she cried out—"Tommy—come out here, the ladies and gentlemen wish to see you." Tommy kept still—said nothing though he heard his mother's call. The mother said again putting in her surliest tone—"Tommy—Tommy, come, come out here the ladies and gentlemen very much want to see you." Tommy grunted and rolled over, somewhat vexed at the calls and said sharply—"Mother—damn it—let me alone till I f—k this damned old she cat and get her with kitten."[54]

When Herndon and Weik's papers reached print, their book included testimonials to Lincoln's love of sharing good stories heard as well as read.

Returning from off the circuit once he said to Mr. Herndon: "Billy, I heard a good story while I was up in the country. Judge [David] D[avis] was complimenting the landlord on the excellence of his beef. 'I am surprised,' he said, 'that you have such good beef. You must have to kill a whole critter when you want any.' 'Yes,' said the landlord, 'we never kill less than a whole critter.'"[55]

1888

27 AUGUST. As the ranks of those who had known Lincoln thinned, lecturers tried to recall his stories. William B. Wilson, who had headed the army's telegraph office early in the war, in lecturing before Philadelphia's United Service Club, told how Lincoln used an old

April Fool's joke that Wilson's audience could have found in Book of Anecdotes and Joker's Knapsack *(1871), 221. Wilson, however, said Lincoln had told his version in 1861.*

I told the President that General McClellan was on his way from Arlington to Fort Cochrane, that our pickets still held Ball's and Bailey's Cross Roads and that no firing had been heard since sunset. The President then inquired if any firing had been heard *before* sunset, and upon my replying there had been none reported laughingly said, "That puts me in mind of a party who, in speaking of a freak of nature, described it as a child who was black from the hips down, and, upon being asked the color from the hips up, replied *black,* as a matter of course."[56]

Besides that one, Wilson's notes, which are now in the Huntington Library, include other anecdotes:

[Responding to fires in Washington, a New Jersey fire brigade offered their services. The president] replied gravely and as if he had just awakened to the true impact of the visit, "Ah yes gentleman but it is a mistake to suppose that I am at the head of the fire department of Washington, I am simply the President of the United States."

[The president greets the telegraphers:] "Morning, what news?" Responding to the salutation I replied "good news because none" whereupon he rejoined "Ah, my young friend That rule doesn't always hold good for a fisherman don't consider it good luck when he can't get a bite."

[26 September 1861 was proclaimed as a fast day and observed by the army except for buttery boy George, who was busily preparing the butteries when shortly after noon the president came in:] Spying George he accosted him with "Well Sonny mixing the juices eh?" Then taking a seat in a large arm chair and adjusting his spectacles he became aware that we were very busy. A smile broke over his face as he saluted us with "Gentlemen this is a fast day and I am pleased to observe that you are working as fast as you can. The proclamation was mine and that is my interpretation of its bearing upon you."[57]

[Having eluded a fire, Lincoln said to Seward:] "By jings, Governor, we are here." Mr Seward . . . in a manner of semi-reproof said, "Mr. President where did you learn that inelegant expression? Without replying Mr. Lincoln turned to us and said "Young gentlemen excuse me for swearing before you 'By Jings' is swearing—for my good old mother taught me that anything that had a 'by' before it is swearing. I wont do so any more."[58]

1890

Henry B. Whipple, great reformer of U.S. Indian policy, remembered how Lincoln had used a story to reassure him that Indian agents would be restrained.

In those early days my visits to Washington were oft-repeated stories of blighted hopes. I found President Lincoln a willing listener. I told him the story of the massacre of 1862, when 300 miles of our border was one track of blood. As I repeated the story of specific acts of dishonesty, the President said: "Did you ever hear of the Southern man who bought monkeys to pick cotton? They were quick; their long, slim fingers would pull out the cotton faster than negroes; but he found it took two overseers to watch one monkey. This Indian business needs ten honest men to watch one Indian agent."[59]

1892

Henry C. Whitney, an Urbana lawyer who rode the circuit with Lincoln in the 1850s, supplied Herndon and Weik with several stories and retained several more for his own book, Life on the Circuit with Lincoln, *based on such events as an alleged practical joke Lincoln pulled on fellow circuit riders. As they approached Salt Creek, Logan County, Lincoln warned that the creek might be flooded. After bundling their clothes on their heads and riding naked through the hot sun they found hardly enough water "to house a frog."[60] Whitney renders the incident to shreds but redeems himself with a classic bon mot.*

I never heard him narrate but one story in a speech, which was this: "A man on foot, with his clothes in a bundle, coming to a running stream which he must ford, made elaborate preparations by stripping off his garments, adding them to his bundle, and, tying all to the top of a stick, which enabled him to raise the bundled high above his head to keep them dry during the crossing. He then fearlessly waded in and carefully made his way across the rippling stream, and found it in no place up to his ankles."

There was a small merchant in Chicago, whom (to suppress his real name) I will call Blower, and who sold out his store and embraced the trade, or profession, of politics. Lincoln had great contempt for him, although he gave him an office; but he said to me one day: "That Blower can compress the most words in the fewest ideas of any man I ever knew."[61]

1895

Another veteran of the telegraph office the president frequented during the war, Harry B. Chandler recalled how Major Thomas Eckert and the president swapped stories. Lincoln teased that the major never came to the office except when there was money to count. The major said it was a coincidence that reminded him of a story about a stylish tailor passing by a shop when the owner "gave a long blow" at the conceited tailor. The indignant tailor said, "I'll teach you not to blow when I'm passing." The shopkeeper said, "I'll teach you not to pass while I'm blowing." That old joke had been in Shakespeare's Jests of *1767 (57). Lincoln topped it with another from 1789, more recently in George Wilkes's* Spirit of the Times, *14 December 1861, 231.*

The President said that [Eckert's story] was very good—very like a story which he had heard of a man who was driving through the country in an open buggy, and was caught at night in a pouring shower of rain. He was hurrying forward toward shelter as fast as possible; passing a farmhouse, a man, apparently struggling with the effects of bad whisky, thrust his head out of the window and shouted loudly, "Hullo! hullo!" The traveller stopped and asked what was wanted. "Nothing of you," was the reply. "Well, what in the d——do you shout hullo for when people are passing!" angrily asked the traveller. "Well, what in the d—— are you passing for when people are shouting hullo!"[62]

Dorothy Lamon Teillard published miscellaneous posthumous papers of her father, Ward Lamon, as Recollections of Abraham Lincoln. *The stories Lincoln is supposed to have told seem derived from reading rather than experience, but two extracts are probably authentic. In the first, accused of embezzling forty dollars from company funds, an officer appealed for a pardon on the grounds that he stole only thirty dollars. The president answered with an anecdote:*

That reminds me of a man in Indiana, who was in a battle of words with a neighbor. One charged that the other's daughter had three illegitimate children. "Now," said the man whose family was so outrageously scandalized, "that's a lie, and I can prove it, for she only has two."

The second extract is about General James B. Fry, provost marshal in charge of army recruiting. Fry had contributed to Allen Thorndike Rice's collection, Reminiscences of President Lincoln, *such bon mots as the president's denying to interfere in a soldier's grievance, "I cannot meddle in your case. I could as easily bail out the Potomac River with a teaspoon as attend to all the details of the army."[63] One would have expected Fry to have contributed our next story also. Fry is supposed to have transmitted a northern governor's complaints about the draft. The president reassured him that the governor was like the boy at a ship-launching employed to crawl under the keel and knock out the trigger, then lie flat and keep still while the ship slid over him.*

The boy did everything right; but he yelled as if he were being murdered from the time he got under the keel until he got out. I thought the skin was all scraped off his back; but he wasn't hurt at all. The master of the yard told me that this boy was always chosen for that job, that he did his work well, that he never had been hurt, but that he always squealed in that way. That's just the way with Governor —— . . . He only wants to make you understand how hard his task is, and that he is on hand performing it.

For her privately printed second edition, Teillard added a stray note of her father's that seems to have been overlooked for the first edition.

On another occasion Mr. Lincoln said that the claim that the Mexican War was not aggressive reminded him of the farmer who asserted, "I ain't greedy 'bout land, I only just wants what jines mine."[64]

1896

In an article syndicated by the American Press Association, Jesse Weik published two more Lincoln stories from David H. Bates, the telegrapher.

During one of his visits to Chicago . . . in the summer of 1858 . . . he was sitting with his host and family on the front veranda facing a small park one evening when he noticed among the children a little fellow who was fat and exceptionally short of stature. "That boy," he observed roguishly, "reminds me of a man named [Enoch] Moore in Springfield, who suffered the loss of both feet in a railroad accident and whose legs are now so short that when he walks in the snow the seat of his trousers wipes up his footprints."

Another letter was from a Catholic priest asking him to suspend the sentence of a man ordered put to death. "If I don't suspend it tonight," he observed, "the man will surely be suspended tomorrow."[65]

Ordnance officer Horace Porter's Campaigning with Grant *included a story that Lincoln undoubtedly heard from his predecessor as Congress's star storyteller, Thomas Corwin of Ohio.*[66] *Porter said that they were discussing a new powder about the size of a walnut developed for fifteen-inch guns. The president examined it with care, then told how before the days of newspapers, country storekeepers would advertise in the meetinghouse before the preacher arrived.*

One evening a man rose up and said: "Brethren, let me take occasion to say, while we're a-waitin', that I have jest received a new inv'ice of sportin' powder. The grains are so small you kin sca'cely see 'em with the naked eye, and polished up so fine you kin stand up and comb yer ha'r in front of one o' them grains jest like it was a lookin' glass. Hope you'll come down to my store at the cross-roads and examine the powder for yourselves." When he had got about this far a rival powder-merchant in the meeting, who had been boiling over with indignation at the amount of advertising the opposition powder was getting, jumped up and cried out, "Brethren, I hope you'll not believe a single word Brother Jones has been sayin' about that powder. I've been down thar and seen it for myself, and I pledge you my word that the grains is bigger than the lumps in a coal-pile; and any one of you, brethren, ef you was in your future state could put a bar'l o' that powder on your shoulder and march squar' through the sulphurious flames surroundin' you without the least danger of an explosion."[67]

1912

John Nicolay's daughter Helen worked from her father's notes for his unfinished biography of Lincoln to compile a volume of her own, Personal Traits of Abraham Lincoln. *She included what one can only assume was a version of a popular story that the editors called so "old but good" that they had printed it twice, without Lincoln, in* Harper's New Monthly Magazine—*in 1858 and again in 1868.*

Then there were the stories in which subjects considered too sacred or too profane were introduced. One described a rough frontier cabin, with children running wild, and a hard-worked wife and mother, slatternly and unkempt, not overhappy perhaps, but with a woman's loyal instinct to make the best of things before a stranger. Into this setting strode an itin-erant Methodist, unctious and insistent, selling Bibles as well as preach-ing salvation. She received him with frontier hospitality, but grew restive under questioning she deemed intrusive, and finally answered rather sharply that of course they owned a Bible. He challenged her to produce it. A search revealed nothing. The children were called to her aid, and at last one of them unearthed and held up for inspection a few tattered leaves. Protest and reproaches on the part of the visitor, but on her own stanch sticking to her colors. "She had no idea," she declared, "that they were so nearly out."[68]

CHAPTER 4

STORIES TOLD BY OTHERS AFTER APRIL 1865

1865

Legendary reporter Albert Richardson, author of best-selling books about his secret ventures into the South as a correspondent for the New York Tribune, *visited the president, who reminded him of a story told by a mutual friend named Hatterscheit.*

He bought a pony of an Indian who could not speak much English but who, when the bargain was completed, said: "Oats—no! Hay—no! Corn—no! Cottonwood—yes! Very much!" Hatterscheit thought this was mere drunken maundering, but a few nights after, he tied his horse in a stable built of cottonwood logs, fed him with hay and corn, and went quietly to bed. The next morning he found the grain and fodder untouched, but the barn was quite empty, with a great hole on one side, which the pony had gnawed his way through. Then he comprehended the old Indian's fragmentary English.[1]

Hard-drinking George Augustus Sala, an English visitor, was a comic illustrator and special correspondent for Charles Dickens's Household Words. *He recorded his impressions of the president as "so tall you might ask, 'How cold the weather was up there.'"*

A lady burst in upon Abraham Lincoln, just as a cabinet council was about to sit. "Mr. President," she exclaimed, "you *must* hear me. You must give me a colonel's commission for my son. Sir, my grandfather fought at

Lexington. My uncle was the only man who didn't run at Bladensburg. Sir, my father fought at New Orleans, and my husband was killed at Monterey." "I guess, madam," Mr. Lincoln is reported to have replied, "your family has done enough for the country; and I'd rather not have any more of 'em."[2]

1866

From the New York Historical Society, where his father, brother, and nephew served successively as librarians, indefatigable and self-effacing Frank Moore compiled a half-dozen anthologies of news-paper clippings, speeches, songs, verse, and anecdotes of the Revolution and Civil War, most notably the twelve volumes of Rebellion Records *(1867). Page references in brackets, however, are to his* Anecdotes, Poetry, and Incidents of the War *(1866).*

In reply to an inquiry whether Mr. Lincoln could trace his ancestry to . . . early families of his own name, Mr. Lincoln with a characteristic face-tiousness, replied that he could not say that he ever had an ancestor older than his father. [28]

To an intimate friend who addressed him always by his own proper title, "Now call me Lincoln, and I'll promise not to tell of the breach of etiquette—if you won't—and I shall have a resting spell from Mister Lincoln."[3] [489]

A lieutenant, whom debts compelled to leave his fatherland . . . was promised a lieutenant's commission in a cavalry regiment. He was so enraptured with his success, that he deemed it a duty to inform the President that he belonged to one of the oldest noble houses in Germany. "O, never mind that," said Mr. Lincoln, "You will not find that to be an obstacle to your advancement." [269–70]

During a conversation on the approaching election in 1864, a gentleman remarked to President Lincoln that nothing could defeat him but Grant's capture of Richmond, to be followed by his nomination in Chicago and acceptance. "Well," said the President, "I feel very much like the man who said he didn't want to die particularly, but if he had got to die, that was precisely the disease he would like to die of." [447]

A Western farmer sought the President day after day until he procured the much desired audience. He had a plan for the successful prosecution of the war, to which Mr. Lincoln listened as patiently as he could. When he was through, he asked the opinion of the President upon his plan. "Well," said Mr. Lincoln, "I'll answer by telling you a story. . . . Mr. Blank of Chicago was an immense loafer . . . in fact, never did anything in his life. One day he got crazy over a great rise in the price of wheat, upon which many wheat speculators gained large fortunes. Blank started off one morning to one of the most successful wheat speculators, and with much enthusiasm laid before him a plan by which he (Blank) was certain of becoming independently rich. When he had finished, he asked the opinion of the hearer upon his plan of operations. The reply came as follows: 'My advice is that you stick to your business.' 'But,' asked Blank, 'What is my business?' 'I don't know, I am sure, what it is,' says the merchant; 'but whatever it is, I advise you to stick to it.'" [510]

FEBRUARY. *"The Editor's Drawer,"* Harper's New Monthly Magazine *32 (1866): 405, said, "Since the assassination of the late much-lamented President, 'Old Abe's jokes' have naturally been but little in vogue," then printed one related by telegrapher Albert B. Chandler about how the whining cry of a newsboy reminded the president of a joke Chicago newsboys once played on him. Chandler himself told a similar story in* The Independent, *4 April 1895, which is just as doubtful.*

"Well," said Mr. Lincoln, "soon after I was nominated for President at Chicago, I went up one day, and one of the first really distinguished men who waited on me was a picture-man, who politely asked me to favor him with a sitting for my picture. Now at that time there were less photographs of my phiz than at present, and I went straightway with the artist . . . who took one of the most really life-like pictures I have ever seen of myself, from the fact that he gave me no *fixing* nor *positions*. But this stiff, ungovernable hair of mine was sticking every way, very much as it is now, I suppose; and so the operation of his camera was but 'holding the mirror up to nature' [*Hamlet* 3.2.22]. I departed, and did not think of pictures again until that evening I was gratified and flattered at the cry of newsboys who had gone to vending the pictures: 'Ere's yer last picter of Old Abe! He'll look better when he gets his *hair* combed!'"

MARCH. *A contributor to "The Editor's Drawer" in* Harper's New Monthly Magazine *32 (1866): 535, recounts an incident starring Ward Lamon that Lamon himself dated about 1849, when he ripped his pants wrestling before the courthouse opened.*[4]

Before he had time to make any change he was called into court to take up a case. The evidence was finished, and Lamon got up to address the jury, and having on a somewhat short coat his misfortune was rather apparent. One of the lawyers, for a joke, started a subscription paper, which was passed from one member of the bar to another as they sat by a long table fronting the bench, to buy a pair of pantaloons for Lamon, "he being," the paper said, "a poor but worthy young man." Several put down their names with some ludicrous subscription, and finally the paper was laid by someone in front of Mr. Lincoln. . . . He quietly glanced over the paper, and immediately took up his pen and wrote after his name, "I can contribute nothing *to the end in view.*"

> SEPTEMBER. *Another correspondent sent "The Editor's Drawer,"* Harper's Weekly *52 (1866): 535, a story that flourished in jest books such as New York's* American Magazine of Wit *(1808), 186–87, long before the war it talks about. Now the president told it to troops who asked him to transfer an unpleasant colonel.*

This reminds me of a little story. It was in the Mexican war—at the battle of Monterey, I believe— that a little Irish captain from Sangamon County was ordered by his Colonel to a position, so and so, with his Company. After hearing the order, the little Captain straightened up full height, and said: "Colonel, will yez be so kind as to tell that to my min yoursel'; for, by jabers, Colonel, I'm not on spakin' terms wid my Company!"

1867

> MARCH. Harper's Magazine's *"The Editor's Drawer" 36 (1867): 537, recounts how the president responded to a petitioner who insisted that his case be handled by Lincoln rather than some nameless, impatient secretary.*

It recalls a story told to me by [Lorenzo] Sweat, of Maine: A man in his neighborhood had a small bull-terrier that could whip all the dogs of the neighborhood. The owner of a large dog which the terrier had whipped asked the owner of the terrier how it happened that the terrier whipped every dog he encountered? "That," said the owner of the terrier, "is no mystery to me; your dog and other dogs get half through a fight before they are ready; now, *my dog is always mad!*"

MARCH. The same column (537–38) tells how the same petitioner asked Lincoln to release a number of men, women, and children detained by General David Hunter. The president replied with a story from Joseph G. Baldwin's Flush Times of Alabama and Mississippi *(1853) that ends with the old judge fining the whole court, "women and children half price" (168).*

An old Judge had a propensity for fining offenders, no matter what the offense. On one occasion the regular term of court was not long enough to close all the cases and enable the Judge to order fines, so he held an adjourned term for that purpose, and while intently occupied in that agreeable duty the stove-pipe fell; whereupon the Judge, enraged at the interruption, without stopping to learn the cause, called out, "Sheriff, arrest every one in the room! Mr. Clerk, enter a fine against every one of them!" Then, looking through his spectacles and seeing the crowd, his Honor said, "Stop, Mr. Clerk; enter a fine against every one in the room, women and children excepted."

1869

NOVEMBER. The Southern monthly The Land We Love *6 (1869): 79–80, edited by ex-Confederate General Daniel Hill, printed Lincoln's reply to a boast that the Northern army would devour the rebels for breakfast.*

That reminds me of an anecdote. Deacon Slinker, of the Ironside Baptist persuasion, was churched in Illinois for loving whisky too well. He defended himself by declaring that he had taken just one mouthful and no more that day. One of the Ironsiders, who was confident of the drunkenness of the worthy brother, asked by the way of puzzling him, how much one mouthful was. To this Slinker answered: "Well, bretherin' and sistern, I had a curiosity to find that out myself, and so I measured it, and my mouth hilt just a pint!" The mouthful of rebs for breakfast will turn out to be a mouthful after Deacon Slinker's pattern.

1872

Patrician bon vivant Benjamin Ogle Tayloe, a friend of W. H. Harrison and Henry Clay, was Washington's oldest pioneer resident.

He was seventy-two when he died in 1868, and he left his memoirs, In Memoriam, *to be privately printed for friends and family.*

Senator [Solomon] Foot of Vermont, chairman of the committee on the Inauguration, said the committee left one point for Mr. Lincoln's decision. "He responded with an anecdote. . . . It was expected a lawsuit would be decided by the testimony of a stranger, a very respectable-looking man, dressed in black, with a white cravat, and supposed to be a preacher. On being called to the book, and asked whether he would swear or affirm, he replied, "I don't care a damn which."[5]

1875

JUNE. A correspondent assures the "Editor's Drawer" in Harper's New Monthly Magazine *50 (1875): 156, that he had heard Lincoln tell a tale about a little wizened man haranguing an Ohio camp meeting; "but it needs his peculiar voice to give it effect."*

"Brethern and sistern" (I wish you could have heard Mr. Lincoln imitate that squeaking voice) "I rise to norate on toe yo . . . There was Noah, he had three sons—ahem—namelie, Shadadarack, Meshisick, and Bellteezer! They all went in toe Dannel's den, and likewise with them was a lion! Ahem" Here the crowd . . . laughed and turned away. So the speaker, after repeating the above, and yet gaining no attention, closed abruptly in the following manner: "Dear perishing friends, ef you will not hear on toe me on this great subjec, I will only say this, that Squire Nobbs has recently lost a little bay mare with a flaxy mane and tail amen!"

1876

Louis Philippe Albert d'Orleans, Comte de Paris, exiled pretender to the throne of France, having served on McClellan's staff, wrote a popular history of the American Civil War that in English translation reached eight volumes. Discussing Lincoln's response to the threat of British intervention over the Trent Affair, the count included "one of those anecdotes he excelled in telling."

"My father," he said, "had a neighbor from whom he was only separated by a fence. On each side of that fence there were two savage dogs, who kept running backward and forward along the barrier all day, barking and yapping at each other. One day they came to a large opening recently made in the fence. Perhaps you think they took advantage of this to devour each other? Not at all. Scarcely had they seen the gap, when they both ran back, each on his own side, with their tails between their legs. These two dogs are fair representatives of America and England."[6]

1886

MAY–JUNE. Veteran Aaron D. Yocum, an attorney of Hastings, Nebraska, supplied Ward Lamon with two Lincoln stories recollected from the president's visit to the Army of the James before Richmond.

A boy called out: "Say Mr President—be a little shy up there. Your head is above the works and you'll get it shot at."

"Don't be alarmed," said he, "I am sideways to 'em and Jeff Davis hasent a marksman over there capable of so good a shot."

A voice rang out: "Say, Abe, when are you going home?"

"I don't know. Just as soon as General [Ben] Butler gets me a pass, I reckon."

"When you get home give our kind regards to Mother Lincoln and tell her for Heavens Sake to send the Army of the James some long tailed shirts."

"You want just the shirts?" . . . All restraint was lost and amid side splitting peals of laughter and relieving shouts of the men the President rode out forever from the camps of his favorite Army.[7]

1887

Founding editor of the literary monthly Dial, *Francis Fisher Browne of Chicago compiled stories from Lincoln's contemporaries for his* Every-day Life of Abraham Lincoln, *including the exchange with an old Democrat that Lincoln had in 1860 after being nominated the state's Republican candidate for president.*

"So you're Abe Lincoln?"

"That's my name, sir," answered Mr. Lincoln.

"They say you're a self-made man," said the Democrat.

"Well, yes," said Mr. Lincoln, "what there is of me is self-made."

"Well, all I've got to say," observed the old man after a careful survey of the statesman before him, "is, that it was a d—n bad job."[8]

23 JANUARY. In the New York Tribune *Augustus Brandegee recalled how when he was a young Republican congressman from Connecticut his passionate plea for a political favor reminded the president of a young lawyer back home.*

"You remind me of a young lawyer in Sangamon County who had hung out his shingle for a long time without having a client. At last he got one, but feeling very anxious not to lose his first case, he thought he would go down and state it to the justice who was to try it and ascertain in advance what he thought of it. So he went down one Sunday evening and stated it for all it was worth, and concluded by asking the justice how he would probably decide it. 'As you state the case,' replied the justice, 'I should be obliged to decide against you. But you had better bring the case. Probably the other side will make so much worse a showing that I shall have to decide the case in your favor.'"[9]

1897

In the Washington Post *ninety-year-old John M. Palmer, a general from Illinois during the war who became governor and senator, recollected one of my own favorite Lincoln fables.*

A certain Judge [John A.] Krum, a lawyer, had been complaining of the treatment he had received from local judges. He swore he meant to carry his case to the supreme court and humiliate the upstart judge who had decided against him. Mr. Lincoln spoke in his quiet, dry way:

"That makes me think of a story. There was a certain man who dreamed that a treasure was buried, and that to find it he had but to dig in a certain spot. His labors were crowned with success only on condition that he keep silent while he was digging. He began to dig. A terrific battle was waged near him. A naval encounter was fought nearby. Innumerable tried to engage him in conversation. Still he kept silent. A great giant passed, walking very rapidly. The digger did not even turn his head. After a while a dwarf came prancing along, walking as if he were nine feet high.

"'Say,' he said to the digger, 'did a giant pass here?' The digger did not answer. The dwarf repeated his inquiry. No answer. 'Can't you answer a civil question?' asked the dwarf. No answer. 'O, well,' said the dwarf. 'I'll just walk along and overtake him.'

"Then the digger broke the silence. 'The hell you will!' he said."[10]

1898

JANUARY. The Detroit Free Press *interviewed eighty-eight-year-old Richard W. Thompson, congressman from Indiana in the 1840s, who recollected Lincoln's story of a credit report on lawyer-turned-merchant Sam Brown who ordered a large bill of goods. The agent said that Brown was worth $100,000 with these assets:*

"He has a beautiful wife, with black hair and lustrous eyes; I should say she is worth $50,000. He has two children, one a little girl, who is the image of her mother, and the other a bright and amiable boy. The girl is worth at least $25,000 and if the boy were mine you could not buy him for $50,000. Besides these objects of value, Mr. Brown has an old table worth 25 cents, an inkstand worth 10 cents and a pocket-knife worth 5 cents. But, over and above all I have named, Sam has, in the corner of his office, a great big rat hole that is worth looking into."[11]

1899

OCTOBER. George B. Wright, a member of Ohio's wartime Governor David Tod's staff, in "personal recollections" for the Ohio Archaeological and Historical Quarterly *included an anecdote told by others along with the president's own anecdote about an inventor seeking a patent.*

One evening while visiting the White House Mr. Lincoln said, "Look here, Tod, how is it that you spell your name with only one *d*. I married a Todd, but she spelled her name with two *d's*. All of her relations do the same. You are the first Tod I ever knew who spelled his name with so few letters." Mr. Tod, smiling, replied, "Mr. President, God spells His name with only one *d*, and what is good enough for God, is good enough for me." President Lincoln used to repeat this story to some of his intimate friends with great hilarity.

I called on Mr. Lincoln with Governor Tod in the fall of 1863. We found Mr. Lincoln and Secretary of State Seward alone together. After our reception and a short interview on general matters, Governor Tod asked the following question: "Mr. President, how many candidates are there in your cabinet for President?" . . . The President said: "Governor, your question reminds me of an experience I once had when practicing law in Illinois. One day a rather seedy looking man called at my office with a bundle under his arm, and requested to see me privately. I took him into my back room, when he told me he had invented a new auger to turn with a crank instead of the old-fashioned way, and if I approved of it he desired me to procure a patent for him. He unfolded his bundle and exhibited his model. I procured a plank and told him to bore a hole in it. He set the auger and began to turn the crank. But we discovered that he had set the screw the wrong way, and instead of boring itself in, it bore itself *out*."[12]

1901

An editor and power in Pennsylvania Republican politics, Alexander K. McClure had known Lincoln, but he most likely contributed only the introduction to the still-reprinted collection Abe Lincoln's Yarns and Stories, *"edited" by him. Page references in brackets are to Zall,* Abe Lincoln Laughing.

Mr. [Isaac] Roland Diller, who was one of Mr. Lincoln's neighbors in Springfield, tells the following: "I was called to the door one day by the cries of children in the street, and there was Mr. Lincoln, striding by with two of his boys, both of whom were wailing aloud. 'Why, Mr. Lincoln, what's the matter with the boys?' I asked. 'Just what's the matter with the whole world,' Lincoln replied. 'I've got three walnuts, and each one wants two.'" [122]

One of Mr. Lincoln's warm friends was Dr. Robert Boal, of Lacon, Illinois. Telling of a visit [unrecorded] paid to the White House soon after Mr. Lincoln's inauguration, he said: "I . . . remember one story he told me on this occasion. "Tom Corwin, of Ohio . . . met an old man at Alexandria who knew George Washington, and he told Tom that George Washington often swore. Now, Corwin's father had always held the father of our country up as a faultless person and told his son to follow in his footsteps. 'Well,' said Corwin, 'when I heard that George Washington was addicted to the vices and infirmities of man, I felt so relieved that I just shouted for joy.'" [122]

[General McClellan] reminds me of the story of a man out in Illinois who, in company with a number of friends, visited the State penitentiary. They wandered all through the institution and saw everything, but just about the time to depart this particular man became separated from his friends and couldn't find his way out. He roamed up and down one corridor after another, becoming more desperate all the time, when, at last, he came across a convict who was looking out from between the bars of his cell door. Here was salvation at last. Hurrying up to the prisoner he hastily asked: "Say! how do you get out of this place!" [122]

[Seeing that only one member of the cabinet supported his wish to avoid conflict with England over the Trent Affair,] I am reminded . . . of a fellow out in my State of Illinois who happened to stray into a church while a revival meeting was in progress. To be truthful, this fellow was not entirely sober. . . . Drowsiness overcoming him, he went to sleep. Before the meeting closed, the pastor asked the usual question—"Who are on the Lord's side?"—and the congregation arose en masse. When he asked, "Who are on the side of the Devil?" the sleeper was about waking up. He heard a portion of the interrogatory, and, seeing the minister on his feet, arose. "I don't exactly understand the question," he said, "but I'll stand by you, parson, to the last. But it seems to me," he added, "that we're in a hopeless minority." [126]

1902

Thomas Gaines Onstot, who as a boy knew Lincoln in New Salem, prepared reminiscences of the region for surviving pioneers. He included the anecdote about two English dandies visiting the White House and coming upon the president shining his shoes.

"Why, Mr. Lincoln, in London no gentleman blacks his own shoes."

"No?" said old Abe, pausing to spit on the brush, "Whose shoes does he black?"[13]

1903

6 APRIL. James Grant Wilson's speech to New York's Order of the Founders and Patriots of America included Lincoln in an old joke about greeting an asylum inmate, "Excuse me, General Washington but a half hour ago you said you were Columbus," and the inmate replying, "Oh, yes, but that was by another mother." Wilson also told about the president and Secretary Seward being driven over such rough roads that the driver swore more and more as the roads became rougher and rougher.

The President asked, "Are you an Episcopalian?" The driver looked very much astonished. "No," he said . . . "Oh, excuse me," said the President, "I thought you must be an Episcopalian, for you swear just like Seward, and he is a church warden."[14]

1906

FEBRUARY. The poet John McGovern's essay comparing him to George Washington in the National Magazine *stressed Lincoln as more the common man. When son Robert announced he was leaving for Senator Sumner's reception for the poet Longfellow, the president gave his blessing.*

"Go, my son," the President said, "but if you are able to hold a respectable conversation for fifteen minutes with those gentlemen, you'll do more than your father ever did."[15]

1907

After a prolific career as novelist and translator of Victor Hugo and Alexandre Dumas, Henry Llewellyn Williams published Lincolnics *(1906) and* The Lincoln Story-Book, *which is still in print and is a more "judicious" collection that claims such sources as in the samples below—Thomas Pendel, White House usher, for the first, and L. E. Chittenden, Lincoln's register of the treasury, for the second. The first Lincoln story had appeared in Locke's* Nasby Papers *(1864): 35; Crittenden's in* Harper's New Monthly Magazine *5 (September 1852): 558, from a story by Sir Walter Scott, without the dialect.*

The ushers and secret service officials on duty at the Executive Mansion during the war were prone to congregate in a little anteroom and exchange reminiscences. This was directly against instructions by the President. One night . . . suddenly the door opened, and there stood President Lincoln, his shoes in his hand. All the crowd scattered save Pendel. . . . The intruder shook his finger at him and, with assumed ferocity, growled: "Pendel, you people remind me of the boy who set a hen on forty-three eggs . . . and then rushed in and told his mother what he had done. 'But a hen can't set on forty-three eggs,' replied the mother. 'No, I guess she can't, but I just wanted to see her spread herself.'"

[Speaking of a soldier accused of sleeping on sentry duty:] "This soldier's life is as valuable to him as any person's in the land. It reminds me of the old Scotch woman's saying about her laird going to be beheaded for participation in a jacobite rebellion: 'It waur na mickle of a head, but it is the only head the puir body ha' got.'"[16]

Philadelphia financier Jay Cooke recollected riding with the president, 21 August 1861, along with Attorney General Edward Bates, whose beard began to turn gray even though the hair on his head "retained an almost youthful appearance."

I begged for an explanation. Mr. Lincoln here remarked, with a quizzical look across to Mr. Bates . . . "Well," said Mr. Lincoln, "it could hardly be otherwise and the cause is that he uses his jaws more than he does his brains." We all laughed heartily at this impromptu and original joke at Mr. Bates's expense and, as I gave the substance . . . to some newspaper men the next day it was published far and wide as one of Mr. Lincoln's original sayings.[17]

David Homer Bates served with A. C. Chandler and C. A. Tinker in the War Department telegraph office, where Lincoln visited routinely during the war. There he shared stories old, new, and borrowed, including these few samples from Bates's Lincoln in the Telegraph Office, *referenced by page numbers in brackets. In the first, after finishing a batch of telegrams, Lincoln says it reminds him of a little girl who ate too much at a party, topped off with raisins for dessert, and threw up during the night. The physician came, Lincoln went on:*

The genial doctor, scrutinizing the contents of the vessel, noticed some small black objects that had just appeared, and remarked to the anxious parent that all danger was past, as the child was "down to the raisins." So when I reach the message in this pile which I saw on my last visit, I know that I need go no further. [41]

In the second sample, Bates described Lincoln swapping stories. Someone recounts a sketch from Tom Hood's Hood's Own *(2d ser., 1861, 415–17) about a baby in an armchair covered with a shawl to protect him from the sun. A fussy nearsighted aunt sits on him, mashing him flat. This reminded Lincoln of an analogue.*

Scene, a theater; curtain just lifted; enter a man with a high silk hat in his hand. He becomes so interested in the movements on the stage that involuntarily he places his hat, open side up, on the adjoining seat without seeing the approach of a fat dowager who, near-sighted, like the fat aunt of the spoiled child, does not observe the open door of the hat. She sits down, and there is a crunching noise, and the owner of the spoiled hat reaches out to rescue his property as the fat woman rises, and holding the hat in front of him says: "Madam, I could have told you that my hat would not fit before you tried it on." [415–17]

Bates's third sample retells a variant of an old anecdote that had appeared in the American Jest Book *of 1789 (61).*

[C. A.] Tinker records that one day Secretary Seward, who was not renowned as a joker, said he had been told that a short time before, on a street crossing, Lincoln had been seen to turn out in the mud to give a colored woman a chance to pass. "Yes," said Lincoln, "it has been a rule of my life that if people would not turn out for me, I would turn out for them. Then you avoid collisions." [204]

The last sample from Bates's collection quotes from a banquet address that his old colleague Tinker gave in Washington on 11 October 1906.

I think I had the pleasure of hearing what in all probability was the last anecdote ever told by Mr. Lincoln in the telegraph office. Early on the morning of April 13, 1865, the day before his assassination . . . I was copying a despatch . . . couched in very laconic terms. He read over the despatch, and after taking in the meaning of the terse phrases, turned to me and, with his accustomed smile, said: "Mr. Tinker, that reminds me of the old story of the Scotch country girl on her way to market with a basket of eggs for sale. She was fording a small stream in scant costume, when a wagoner approached from the opposite bank and called, 'Good morning, my lassie; how deep's the brook, and what's the price of eggs?' 'Knee deep and a sixpence,' answered the little maid, who gave no further attention to her questioner." [206]

1908

In his Memoirs Californian *congressman Cornelius Cole recounts that when he and fellow congressman Thomas Shannon badgered the president for a favor, his defense was an anecdote about the early days in Springfield when there were only the Methodist, Presbyterian, and Baptist churches. A brash Universalist preacher tried to set up a church of his own. The local preachers decided to take turns putting down the intruder.*

It fell to the lot of the Presbyterian dominie to preach the first sermon, and he began by reminding his hearers how happily they were getting along in Springfield, spiritually and otherwise. "And now," he said, "there comes among us a stranger, to establish a church on the belief that all men are to be saved, but my brethren let us hope for better things."[18]

1909

FEBRUARY–MARCH. James Grant Wilson published Lincoln's oft-repeated story of the perfect wife in "Recollections of Lincoln," Putnam's Monthly and the Reader *5 (1909): 673.*

Among several good things, the President told of a Southern Illinois preacher who, in the course of his sermon, asserted that the Saviour was the only perfect man . . . also, that there was no record in the Bible, or elsewhere, of any perfect woman having lived on earth. Whereupon there arose in the rear of the church a persecuted-looking personage who, the parson having stopped speaking, said: "I know a perfect woman, and I've heard of her about every day for the last six years." "Who was she?" asked the minister. "My husband's first wife."[19]

4 FEBRUARY. David Homer Bates supplied Leslie's Weekly *with an instance of Lincoln using humor as a release valve by talking about bizarre patents. The first patent, for a hen walker, had been in* Harper's Weekly *1 (16 June 1857): 366.*

In July 1864, upon Lincoln's return to the War Department after the battle of Fort Stevens, in which the total number of killed and wounded on both sides was nearly one thousand, he gave us a pretty full account of the fighting, and then told two stories, both relating to applications for letters patent. The first device, called a "hen walker," was intended to prevent hens from scratching up the garden, and consisted of a movable brace attached to the hen's legs so that at each scratch the hen was propelled forward, and so by successive scratches all the way out of the garden. The other device was called a "double-back-action hen persuader," which was so adjusted under the hen's nest that as each egg was laid it fell through a trap door out of sight of the author, who would then be persuaded to lay another egg.[20]

12 FEBRUARY. The Los Angeles Times *devoted page 8 to commemorating Lincoln's centenary, including a fresh anecdote.*

He had appointed to a South American consulate an Ohio young man who was very much the dandy. The appointee, dressed in gorgeous style, was on his way to the White House to thank the President for his appointment, when he encountered an acquaintance who liked a joke as well as he knew the tropics. "Sorry for you, awfully sorry," he told the rejoicing young consul. "Why, down there, they have bugs that'll bore holes clean through you before you've been consul a week." It took out of the appointee all the starch except what he had in his shirt. When he saw the President, it was a downcast visitor who said to Lincoln: "Mr. President, I can't say I'm so very glad of this appointment, after all. Why, I hear they have bugs down there that are liable to eat me up inside of a week." Lincoln meditated: then—"Well, young man, if they do, they'll leave behind a mighty good suit of clothes."

12 FEBRUARY. In a Lincoln's birthday speech at Pontiac, Illinois, old friend Richard Price Morgan of Bloomington recounted two anecdotes. He claimed that Lincoln told a story about state treasurer John Moore. But if Lincoln did tell him the story, he was fooling Morgan, for it had been a perennial jest book favorite since at least 1617, when it appeared about a "John Lawrence" in a temperance tract by Thomas Young, England's Bane *(sig. F2).*

Speaking of the relative merits of New England rum and corn juice, as he called it, to illuminate the human mind he told me this story of John Moore, who resided south of Blooming Grove, and subsequently became state treasurer. Mr. Moore came to Bloomington one Saturday in a cart drawn by a fine pair of red steers. For some reason he was a little late starting home, and besides his brown jug, he otherwise had a good load on. In passing through the grove that night, one wheel of the cart struck a stump or root and threw the pole out of the ring of the yoke. The steers, finding themselves free, ran away, and left John Moore sound asleep in his cart, where he remained all night. Early in the morning, he roused himself, and looking over the side of the cart and around in the woods, he said: "If my name is John Moore, I've lost a pair of steers. If my name ain't John Moore, I've found a cart." After a good laugh together, Lincoln said: "Morgan, if you ever tell this story, you must add that Moore told it on himself."

Don and Virginia Fehrenbacher (Recollected Words, 336) doubt the authenticity of Morgan's next quotation, which he claims to have repeated since Lincoln first said it in Bloomington in 1856. J. G. Nicolay and John Hay (Complete Works, 3:349n) reported that the Chicago Tribune and the Brooklyn Eagle could find no record of his ever saying it. As if in response, Morgan offers concrete details in place of a paper trail.

I stood next to Mr. Lincoln and heard him say: "You can fool some of the people all of the time, and all of the people some of the time, but you can't fool all of the people all of the time." He was addressing an assemblage of three or four hundred people from the raised platform of the entrance to the Pike House, in Bloomington, upon the subject of the Kansas-Nebraska Act, and reviewing the arguments of Douglas in support of it. His application of his epigram was so apt and so forcible that I have never forgotten it, and I believe no verbal modification of it would be accurate.[21]

MARCH. Prolific James Grant Wilson, "Recollections of Lincoln," in Putnam's Monthly and Reader included the anecdote about a resplendent astronaut but I prefer the version in the stenographic report of his speech to the Lincoln Fellowship of New York, 1911, as probably closer to Lincoln's way of telling a story.

I do not remember what led up to it, but something, for he rarely told a story [without a purpose]—something led him to speak of New Orleans. He said when he was there—it was many years before the war, the days of slavery, when he was there there was a man making an ascent in a balloon, which created a great deal of excitement in New Orleans. He went one day to see the man go up; the wind was rather too strong, for this fellow instead of coming down as he intended to, he was blown away some miles into the country, and finally he affected landing in a cornfield, where there was a gang of slaves at work, and when they saw this thing coming apparently from heaven, these darkies all took to the woods, except one rheumatic old darky, who could not run, and could hardly walk, so he stood his ground, and this figure, gorgeous in spangles and so forth, and the old circus clothes, as General Sickles remembers, climbed out of the balloon, and came towards the old darky, who thought he would try to do the best he could for himself, so he said, "Good morning, good morning, Master Jesus, how is your papa?"[22]

1910

19 JANUARY. At its Lincoln centennial exercises, the Brookline Histori-cal Society heard reminiscences of William J. Seaver, who as clerk in the general store during 1856–57 had known him in Springfield. Seaver's fellow clerks, criticizing a customer for her lack of tact and sophistication, concurred that she had better qualities—triggering this remark from Lincoln:

"That reminds me of a girl who wasn't much of a dancer. Her friends said that what she lacked in dancing she made up in turning round."[23]

After the death of street railway tycoon Thomas Lowry in February 1909, his family published his memoirs in an edition of 100 copies pri-vately printed. In our first sample, Lowry related how with his father, a Pleasantville, Illinois, farmer, he had visited Lincoln. Page references in brackets are to Lowry's Reminiscences of Abraham Lincoln.[24]

He received us very cordially, and among other things told us of his last visit to David F. Lowry, my uncle in Pekin, Illinois, where he usually stopped when "travelling the circuit." Mr. Lincoln said: "As I was going up the path from the street to the house, some boys were playing marbles near the walk. I stopped and put my hand on the head of Mr. Lowry's boy and said: 'My boy, you're playing marbles!' The urchin looked up and replied, 'Any d—n fool ought to see that.'" [11–12]

Another sample from Lowry's book relates the popular joke about how long a man's legs should be. Lowry added that Owen Lovejoy told it to him as a student at the Galesburg college in 1863–64.

It was when Lincoln, Stephen A. Douglas, and Owen Lovejoy were travel-ling in a stage coach on their way to attend Court at Bloomington, Illi-nois. Douglas had a *very* long body and very short legs, being only five feet high; Lovejoy had a short body, and long legs proportionately, and all know Lincoln's build. Douglas chaffed Lovejoy about his long legs and pot belly and Lovejoy retorted as to his very short legs, etc. One of them asked Lincoln: "How long should a man's legs be in proportion to his body?" and Lincoln replied: "I have not given the matter much consideration, but at first blush I should judge they ought to be long enough to reach from the body to the ground." [23]

—Another story which was attributed to Lincoln in those days and afterwards diverted to others, was that of Lincoln riding on horseback and coming to an overturned load of hay. The boy driving the team was quite "upset," and striving hard to right the load. Lincoln asked the boy to go with him to a farmhouse where he could get some help. After much persuasion the boy consented, and after lunch he said: "Dad won't like my being away so long," and started back to his load of hay. Lincoln said: "Don't hurry; I'll send some help back to aid you." The lad replied: "Don't you know that dad's under that hay?" [24–25]

Lincoln told my father about his first speech in Congress. He said he was always embarrassed when he got up to talk, and he felt in Congress about as elsewhere. He illustrated it by saying he felt like the boy whose teacher asked him why he didn't spell better. The boy replied, "Cause I hain't just got the hang of the school-house, but I'll get on better later." [25]

The simple, colloquial humor of Lincoln stories made them a fine fit for school readers, as in Stanley Schell's Lincoln Celebrations.

A lawyer, opposed to Lincoln, was trying to convince a jury that precedent was superior to law, and that custom made things legal in all cases. Lincoln rose to answer him. He told the jury he would argue the case in the same way. He said: "Old Squire Bagly, from Menard, came into my office and said, 'Lincoln, I want your advice as a lawyer. Has a man what's been elected a justice of the peace a right to issue a marriage license?' I told him he had not; when the old Squire threw himself back in his chair very indignantly, and said, 'Lincoln, I thought you was a lawyer. Now, Bob Thomas and me had a bet on this thing, and we agreed to let you decide; but if this is your opinion, I don't want it, for I know a thunderin' sight better, for I have been squire now for eight years and have done it all the time.'"[25]

1911

11 FEBRUARY. At the Lincoln Fellowship Dinner, New York, former postmaster general Horatio C. King spoke about Lincoln's pleasure when old friends would visit to swap stories old and new.

As this particular gentleman was about to leave he said to Mr. Lincoln, "I want you to be honest with me. How do you like being president of the United States?" Well, Mr. Lincoln smiled and looked at him and then said, "You have heard the story, haven't you, about the man as he was ridden out of town on a rail, tarred and feathered, somebody asked him how he liked it, and his reply was if it was not for the honor of the thing, he would much rather walk."[26]

1912

A quarter century after his death, David K. Cartter, chief justice of the District of Columbia supreme court, 1863–87, was finally cited by Anthony Gross's Lincoln Story Book *as a source of a Lincoln law story. A humorist himself, Cartter said that Millard Fillmore made his reputation as conservative and wise by "never swearing in company, always wearing a clean shirt and never uttering a sentiment that the asses around him did not at once recognize as an old acquaintance."[27]*

Lincoln told a story of James Quarles, a distinguished lawyer of Tennessee. Quarles, he said, was trying a case, and after producing his evidence rested; whereupon the defense produced a witness who swore Quarles completely out of court, and a verdict was rendered accordingly. After the trial one of his friends came to him and said: "Why didn't you get that feller to swar on your side!" "I didn't know anything about him," replied Quarles. "I might have told you about him," said the friend, "for he would swar for you jest as hard as he'd swar for the other side. That's his business. Judge, that feller takes in swarin' for a livin'."[28]

The Lincoln Story Book *also printed Lincoln's literary criticism adapted from Artemus Ward's mock testimonial: "For people who like the kind of lectures you deliver, they are just the kind of lectures such people like."*

Robert Dale Owen, the spiritualist, once read the President a long manuscript on an abstruse subject with which that rather erratic person loved to deal. Lincoln listened patiently until the author asked for his opinion, when he replied with a yawn: "Well, for those who like that sort of thing I should think it is just the sort of thing they would like."[29]

Celebrated singer Lillie de Hegerman-Lindencrone's memoir reprinted her July 1864 letter about meeting the president.

Mr. Lincoln said, "I think I might become a musician if I heard you often, but so far I know only two tunes."

"*Hail Columbia*?" I asked. "You know that, I am sure."

"Oh, yes; I know that, for I have to stand up and take off my hat."

"And the other one?"

"The other one? Oh, the other one is the other when I don't stand up."[30]

1920

A native Kentuckian and Speaker of the House of Representatives during World War One, Champ Clark's memoirs, appearing a year after he died, included a Lincoln anecdote.

He generally sat in a rickety old chair in the White House. One of his visitors said, "Mr. President, that is a bad chair. You should have a better one." "Yes," he replied, "this is a bad chair, but, bad as it is, I am inclined to believe that I know several statesmen who are perfectly willing to occupy it."[31]

1922

Baptist minister, lawyer, and legendary lecturer for sixty years, Russell H. Conwell founded Temple University for working people in 1884. His book, Why Lincoln Laughed, *described a visit twenty years earlier with the president that Don and Virginia Fehrenbacher found suspect, but which covered the range of Lincoln stories. Page numbers refer to the edition published by Harper and Brothers in 1922.*

One day when I was at the White House . . . a man bustled in self-importantly and whispered something to him. As the man left the room Lincoln turned to me and smiled. . . . "He's the biggest liar in Washington. You can't believe a word he says. He reminds me of an old fisherman I used to know who got such a reputation for stretching the truth that he bought a pair of scales and insisted on weighing every fish in the presence of witnesses. One day a baby was born next door, and the doctor borrowed the fisherman's scales to weigh the baby. It weighed forty-seven pounds." [4]

[Reminded that during the Cooper Union speech he had forgotten to remove the pencil behind his ear:] He said that his absent-mindedness on that occasion recalled to him the story of the Englishman who was so absent-minded that when he went to bed he put his clothes carefully into the bed and threw himself over the back of his chair. [16]

[Artemus] Ward once stated that Lincoln told him that he was an expert at raising corn to fatten hogs, but, unfortunately for his creditors, they were his neighbor's hogs. [52]

According to Conwell, Lincoln passed off an old joke as one of Ward's. It was an anecdote about "Uncle Ben" that had appeared in the Spirit of the Times *(2 May 1857).*

"Ward told Mr. [Salmon] Chase that his father was an artist who was true to life, for he made a scarecrow so bad that the crows brought back the corn they had stolen two years before." [74]

1924

In Personal Reminiscences, *a twenty-three-page pamphlet privately printed in sixty-five copies at Moline, Illinois, Judge George W. Shaw recollected Lincoln's debates with Douglas.*

His ideas were clearly and forcibly expressed. He said: "They tell me that if the Republicans prevail, slavery will be abolished, and whites will marry and form a mongrel race. Now, I have a sister-in-law down in Kentucky, and if any one can show me that if Fremont is elected she will have to marry a negro, I will vote against Fremont, and if that isn't an argumentum ad hominem it is an argument ad womanum." The joke never failed to bring down the house. [18]

1926

Smith Stimmel's Personal Recollections of Abraham Lincoln *(26–27) featured Lincoln's reply to the soldiers who complained that his bodyguard would be of more use at the front.*

"You boys remind me of a farmer friend of mine in Illinois, who said he could never understand why the Lord put the curl in a pig's tail. It never seemed to him to be either useful or ornamental, but he reckoned that the Almighty knew what he was doing when he put it there. I don't think

I need guards, but Mr. Stanton . . . thinks I do, and as it is in his department, if you go to the front he will insist upon others coming from the front to take your place."[32]

1926–27

The Journal of the Illinois State Historical Society *published the memoirs of Elizabeth Todd Grimsley, Mary Lincoln's cousin and bridesmaid who went with the family to Washington and stayed six months in the White House. She included an exchange between Lincoln and a Tazewell landlady serving supper.*

She turned to Major Stuart, a remarkably handsome cousin of ours, saying, "Stuart, how fine and pert you do look!, but Lincoln, whatever have you been a doing? you do look powerful weak."

"Nothing out of common, Ma'm," was his reply, "but did you ever see Stuart's wife? or did you ever see mine? I just tell you whoever married into the Todd family gets the worst of it."[33]

L. White Busbey's biography of Speaker Joe Cannon included Lincoln's reply at Decatur when "Uncle Joe" asked if he had come to the State Republican Convention, June 1860.

"I'm most too much of a candidate to be here, and not enough of one to stay away."

1939

Ida Tarbell's notes for her popular biography included an undated interview with Rev. Byron Sunderland, the Senate chaplain during Lincoln's administration, recounting a story the president told him during the Trent Affair, 1861. The story later appeared in Harper's New Monthly Magazine *for September 1865 as about Doctor Charles Dyer, Lincoln's commissioner of slave trade.*

It makes me think of an Indian chief that we had out West. He was visited by an Englishman once who tried to impress him with the greatness of England. "Why," said he to the chief, "the sun never sets on England." "Humph!" said the Indian. "I suppose it's because God wouldn't trust them in the dark."[34]

The work of passionate Lincoln collector Emanuel Hertz has been crankily dismissed as "worse than useless" because it is undocumented and indiscriminate.[35] *The scope of his anecdote collection* Lincoln Talks *(New York: Viking Press, 1939), however, was so broad that the law of averages worked for some possibly authentic stories, as referenced in parentheses below and typified by the one about General Edward D. Townsend, Winfield Scott's chief of staff, who died in 1893. Hertz has Townsend tell how the president expressed his confidence in U. S. Grant by alluding to the automaton-chess player popular in the 1850s.*

The automaton was challenged by a celebrated player, who, to his great chagrin, was beaten twice by the machine. At the end of the second game, the player, significantly pointing his finger at the automaton, exclaimed in a very decided tone: "There's a man in it!" And this, sir, is just the secret of our present success. [562]

In attributing the following story to Beecher's Magazine, *Hertz could have meant either the* Independent *or the* Christian Union. *Whatever the case, Henry Ward Beecher wrote a friend that Lincoln had told him three stories—"two of which I forget, and the third won't bear telling."*[36] *Could one of the stories have been Lincoln's reaction to a report about widespread secret traffic with the rebels?*

When I was out West, I knew an old farmer who had moved there, and settled in a dense forest not far from my house. He cleared about an acre of land, built a log cabin, brought his wife and children there, bought a cow, a pig, and some fowls, and seemed to be living very happily and doing finely. He had a truck-patch on most of the cleared ground, on which he was growing his winter store of vegetables. All the trees had been cut down except one old monarch, which he had left to shade his house. It was a majestic looking tree, and apparently perfect in every part—tall, straight, and of immense size—the grand old sentinel of his forest home.

One morning, while at work in his garden, he saw a squirrel run across the ground before him. Thought he, that fellow would make me a nice dinner. So he picked up a stick and sent it flying after him; but squirrel-like he dodged it and went up the great pine tree. The woodman went into the house and got his gun to shoot him. After looking a long time he spied a hole, and thought the tree might be hollow. He proceeded to examine it carefully and, much to his surprise, he found that the stately monarch that he had spared for its beauty and grandeur to be the pride and protection of his little farm was hollow from top to bottom. Only a rim of sound wood remained, barely sufficient to support its weight; all the inside was punky or rotten.

What was he to do? If he cut it down, it would spoil nearly all his truck-patch with its great length and spreading branches. If he let it remain, his family was in constant danger. In a storm it might fall, or the wind might blow it down, and his house and children be crushed by it. What should he do? As he turned away, he said sadly: "I wish I had never seen that squirrel" and, said Mr. Lincoln, "I wish we had never seen what we have today." [363–64]

More than any other single work, the third volume of Carl Sandburg's immensely popular Abraham Lincoln: The War Years *formed the warp and woof of Lincoln's legacy of laughter as we know it. Stories real or imagined, from folklore or print, embedded themselves in national memory wrapped in Sandburg's own prairie idiom. Hearsay was okay—as when Allan Nevins told me of lunching with Sandburg in Chicago. An acquaintance passed by. Sandburg muttered: "He thinks he's Lincoln. He acts like Lincoln. He dresses like Lincoln. He talks like Lincoln. He can't wait to be assassinated." Three samples from* The War Years *are here referenced by page numbers in brackets. Sandburg could have seen the first anecdote in the* Davenport Democrat and Leader *(22 October 1905) as told by Ben Brayton Jr., who in 1857 was the fifteen-year-old of the story.*[37]

In the White House Lincoln philosophized no less than in earlier days, in the same manner as when, after hearing many theories and noisy wranglings in a big law case, he had walked out on the Rock Island bridge, coming on a boy with a fishing-pole whose legs dangled kindly from the ties above the water. "I suppose you know all about this river," he ventured. The boy, brightly: "I guess I do. It was here when I was born, and it's been here ever since." And Lincoln smiled. "I'm mighty glad I walked out here where there is not so much opinion and a little more fact." [321]

The second story from Sandburg had appeared in 1901 as a much longer version by the untrustworthy James Scovel in Overland Monthly *(2d ser., 38:265–67).*

One story James M. Scovel said Lincoln told to illustrate the petty jealousies and bickerings among Congressmen and army generals. Lincoln was reminded of two Illinois men, one Farmer Jones, a churchman gifted in prayer, the other Fiddler Simpkins, welcome at every country merrymaking. At one Wednesday evening prayer meeting Brother Jones made a wonderful prayer which touched the hearts of all. And Brother Simpkins felt called on to rise and say, "Brethring and sistring, I know that I can't make half as good a prayer as Brother Jones, but by the grace of God I can fiddle the shirt off of him." [337]

The final sample of Sandburg's vintage stock has Lincoln retell one of Sydney Smith's most famous anecdotes that had appeared in Smith's four-volume Works *in 1840 (4:392–93).*

"The great West is with you," Ralph Emerson of Rockford, Illinois assured [Lincoln]. "Yes—but I am sometimes reminded of Old Mother Partington on the sea beach. A big storm came up and the waves began to rise till the water came in under her cabin door. She got a broom and went on sweeping it out. But the water rose higher and higher, to her knees, to her waist, at last to her chin. But she kept on sweeping and exclaiming, 'I'll keep on sweeping as long as the broom lasts, and we will see whether the storm or the broom will last the longest.'" [383]

1980

After Sandburg, biographers and historians, along with anthologists, kept Lincoln stories flowing. The popular periodical Smithsonian *for June and August 1980 entertained opinions about which general Lincoln had in mind in a popular story. In 1864 the Confederate press put it this way: "A Yankee puffer having stated that Hooker's head-quarters are in the saddle, the Mobile Advertiser observes: 'To think of a general that didn't know his hindquarters from his headquarters expecting to whip General Lee.'"[38] The* Smithsonian's *version read:*

Lincoln sent General [Joe] Hooker to take over the Army; Hooker rushed headlong into action, sending his despatches from "Headquarters in the saddle." Grinning to an aide, Lincoln said: "The trouble with Hooker is that he's got his headquarters where his hindquarters ought to be."[39]

1994

Surveying Lincoln's reputation, Merrill D. Peterson's Lincoln in American Memory *(New York: Oxford University Press) followed*

Sandburg in neglecting to cite sources for "stories treasured in memory," as this one about Lincoln at a dance. It should not be confused with the one about Lincoln telling Mary he wanted to dance with her in the worst way and she later assuring him that he had done so.[40]

An old-line Whig, torn about the war until the tide shifted to the Union in 1863, came to the President looking for an office. Lincoln was reminded of the time he went to his first dance in Springfield. He bought a new suit of clothes and a new hat. He had such a good time at the dance, he was among the last to leave. When he went to retrieve his hat, he was handed an old, worn one. "This is not mine; I had a new hat," he said. The reply came back: "Mr. Lincoln, the new ones were all gone two hours ago." [100]

2003

David Herbert Donald envisioned Lincoln with Secretary Seward as straight man in "We Are Lincoln Men" (New York: Simon and Schuster). The exchange had been in the New York Post's *"Several Little Stories of or about President Lincoln" on 17 February 1864.*

I like to imagine these two on one of their occasional strolls down Pennsylvania Avenue, unaccompanied by secret service or armed guards, even though they were in the capital of a nation at war. Seward is as usual effervescent and loquacious; Lincoln soft spoken and reserved. But then Lincoln raises his hand to point to a sign overhanging the street: "T.R. Strong."

"Ha!" Lincoln exclaims. "T.R. Strong, but coffee are stronger." [171]

2006

On the morning that I concluded the draft of this book, the postman brought the winter 2006 issue of Phi Beta Kappa's American Scholar, *which concluded with Ted Widmer's exposé of Lincoln's obscenity hidden in "suppressed anecdotes." As evidence, Widmer presented the one from Moses Hampton about razor stropping and another from Christopher Brown on why woman is like a barrel. I suppose that this phenomenon proves once again that there's no such thing as an old Lincoln story. It's new the first time you hear it.*

NOTES

Introduction

1. "Horse's Tale," *Harper's Monthly Magazine* 113 (Sept. 1906): 539.

2. Joseph H. Barrett, *Lincoln and the Presidency,* 2 vols. (Cincinnati: Robert Clarke, 1904), 337n.; *Century Magazine* 74 (Sept. 1907): 809; *Scribner's Monthly Magazine* 15 (Mar. 1878): 679.

3. Harold Holzer, "Avoid Saying Foolish Things," in *We Cannot Escape History,* ed. James McPherson (Urbana: Univ. of Illinois Press, 1995), 112.

4. *Vanity Fair* 3 (28 Feb. 1861): 102.

5. P. M. Zall, *George Washington Laughing* (Hamden: Archon, 1989), xxi–xxii.

6. Diary of Joseph T. Miles, Sept. 1864; Charles M. Segal, ed., *Conversations with Lincoln* (New York: Putnams, 1961), 348.

7. Josephine Metzger to the author, 1974.

8. P. M. Zall, "Abraham Lincoln Laughing," in *The Historians' Lincoln,* ed. Gabor Boritt (Urbana: Univ. of Illinois Press, 1988), 8–9.

9. Mildred Berry, "Abraham Lincoln: His Development in the Skills of the Platform," in *History and Criticism of American Public Address,* ed. W. N. Brigance (New York: Russell and Russell, 1960), 851.

10. Ibid., 857–58.

11. *Chicago Times,* 12 Oct. 1858.

12. Zall, "Abraham Lincoln Laughing," 2–9.

13. Michael Burlingame, ed., *Lincoln's Journalist* (Carbondale: Southern Illinois Univ. Press, 1998), 160.

14. Harry T. Pratt, "Illinois As Lincoln Knew It," in *Papers in Illinois History,* comp. Illinois State Historical Society (Springfield: Illinois State Historical Society, 1938), 139–40.

15. Berry, "Abraham Lincoln: His Development in the Skills of the Platform," 851; see also a similar event at Council Bluffs, Huntington Library (San Marino, CA) MS, HM 39723.

16. William E. Burton, *Cyclopedia of Wit* (New York: Appleton, 1858), 1:537, vs. *Massachusetts Magazine* 1 (June 1789): 383.

17. *Harper's New Monthly Magazine* 6 (Mar. 1853): 565.

18. Augustus John Foster, *Jeffersonian America,* ed. R. B. Davis (San Marino, CA: Huntington Library, 1954), 196.

19. *History of Sangamon County* (Chicago: Interstate, 1881), 209.

20. William V. Pooley, *Settlement of Illinois* (Madison: Univ. of Wisconsin Press, 1908), 570–73.

21. Kenneth J. Winkle, "The Voters of Lincoln's Springfield," *Journal of Social History* 25 (1992): 596.

22. John Linden Rolle, "Sangamo Town," *Journal of the Illinois State Historical Society* 19 (1926–27): 156.

23. *History of Sangamon County,* 499.

24. Abraham Lincoln, *Writings and Speeches,* ed. Don E. Fehrenbacher (New York: Library of America, 1989), 2:208.

25. *Scribner's Monthly* 16 (Oct. 1878): 818.

26. Otto R. Kyle, "Mr. Lincoln Steps Out," *Abraham Lincoln Quarterly* 5 (1948): 37.

27. *Congressional Globe,* 30th Cong., 1st sess., 1042.

28. Ida M. Tarbell, *Life of Abraham Lincoln* (New York: Lincoln History Society), 2:5.

29. *Boston Daily Advertiser,* 14 Sept. 1848.

30. James Schouler, "Abraham Lincoln at Tremont Temple," *Massachusetts Historical Society Proceedings* 42 (1909): 76.

31. Ibid., 86–87.

32. *New York Tribune,* 26 June 1858.

33. Robert Hitt interview, undated, in Huntington Library Scrapbook 151170, 5:64.

34. Paul M. Zall, *Lincoln on Lincoln* (Lexington: Univ. Press of Kentucky, 1999), 103–4; Harold Holzer, *The Lincoln-Douglas Debates* (New York: HarperCollins, 1993), 30.

35. Lincoln, *Writings and Speeches,* 2:68, 137.

36. Harper, *Opposition Press,* 301.

37. Diary of John Lyle King, 8 Jan. 1863, Indiana Historical Society, Indianapolis.

38. Huntington Library MS, HN LN 2408, 2:33.

39. Huntington Library MS, BR Box 281 (22).

40. Ellery Sedgwick, *Happy Profession* (Boston: Little Brown, 1946), 164–65; see also Harold Holzer, *Lincoln at Cooper Union* (New York: Simon and Schuster, 2005), 84–85.

41. Robert Bloom, "As the British Saw Lincoln," *Image of America, Topic Nine* (Washington, PA: Washington and Jefferson College, 1965), 47–48.

42. Berry, "Development," 858.

43. Herbert Mitgang, *Abraham Lincoln, a Press Portrait* (New York: Fordham Univ. Press, 2000), 279–80.

44. Douglas L. Wilson and Rodney O. Davis, *Herndon's Informants* (Urbana: Univ. of Illinois Press, 1998), 350, 541.

45. Don Fehrenbacher and Virginia Fehrenbacher, *Recollected Words of Abraham Lincoln* (Stanford: Stanford Univ. Press, 1996), 53.

46. To Reverdy Johnson, 26 Apr. 1861; Lincoln, *Writings and Speeches,* 2:225–26.

47. Brooks, *Washington in Wartime,* 226.

48. Salmon P. Chase, *Inside Lincoln's Cabinet,* ed. David Donald (London: Longmans, 1954), 149.

49. Benjamin P. Thomas, "Lincoln's Humor, an Analysis," *Papers of the Abraham Lincoln Association* 3 (1981): 45–46.

50. Apr. 30, 1864; John Hay, *Inside Lincoln's White House: Complete Civil War Diary,* ed. Michael Burlingame and John R. T. Ettlinger (Carbondale: Southern Illinois Univ. Press, 1997), 194.

51. Barnaby Zall, Esq., recalled this from his course on "Evidence," George Washington Law School.

Lincoln's Writings and Speeches

1. Michael Burlingame, ed. "Martinette Hardin McKee Recalls Mary Todd," *Lincoln Herald* 97 (Summer 1995): 72; J. Edward Murr, "Lincoln in Indiana," *Indiana Magazine of History* 14 (Mar. 1918): 57; Huntington Library MS, LN 2048 1:148–49.

2. P. M. Zall, *Lincoln on Lincoln* (Lexington: Univ. Press of Kentucky, 1999), 40–43.

3. Ibid., 42–43.

4. P. M. Zall, ed., *Abe Lincoln Laughing* (Knoxville: Univ. of Tennessee Press, 1997), 13–14.

5. *Harper's New Monthly Magazine* 16 (May 1858): 856–57; J. G. Holland, *Life of Abraham Lincoln* (Springfield, MA: Gurdon Bill, 1866), 76.

6. Abraham Lincoln, *Collected Works,* ed. Roy P. Basler, Marion D. Pratt, and Lloyd A. Dunlap, 8 vols. (New Brunswick: Rutgers Univ. Press, 1953–55 and supplements), 1:244.

7. Ibid., 1:275–76.

8. *Congressional Globe,* 30th Cong., 1st sess., 108.

9. Ibid., 710.

10. Huntington Library MS, FAC 118.

11. *Congressional Globe,* 30th Cong., 1st sess., 1042–43.

12. Donald W. Riddle, *Congressman Abraham Lincoln* (Urbana: Univ. of Illinois Press, 1957), 134–35; Lincoln, *Collected Works,* 2:3.

13. Lincoln, *Collected Works,* 2:19.

14. Elwin L. Page, "Franklin Pierce and Abraham Lincoln," *Abraham Lincoln Quarterly* 5 (1949): 458–64.

15. Paul M. Angle, *"There Have I Lived"* (New Brunswick: Rutgers Univ. Press, 1950), 50.

16. Lincoln, *Writings and Speeches,* 1:287–89; "The old woman" echoes her counterpart in the popular jest book *Mrs. Partington's Carpet-Bag of Fun* (New York: Garrett, 1854), 195: "She put the firmest reliance on Providence till the breeching broke, and then she gave up."

17. Zall, *Lincoln on Lincoln,* 304–5; Paul Selby, ed., *Historical Encyclopedia of Illinois* (Chicago: Munsell, 1912), 1:73; Frank R. Stevens, "Life of Douglas," *Journal of the Illinois State Historical Society* 16 (1923–24): 480.

18. Lincoln, *Writings and Speeches,* 1:347–48.

19. Stevens, "Life of Douglas," 487; Robert W. Johannsen, *Lincoln, the South, and Slavery* (Baton Rouge: Louisiana State Univ. Press, 1991), 27.

20. Lincoln, *Writings and Speeches,* 1:348.

21. Paul M. Angle, ed., Isaac N. Phillips, *Abraham Lincoln by Some Men Who Had Known Him* (Chicago: American House, 1950), 63; Zall, *Abe Lincoln Laughing,* 17.

22. Lincoln, *Collected Works,* 2:333.

23. Otto R. Kyle, "Mr. Lincoln Steps Out," 37.

24. Lincoln, *Collected Works,* 2:384.

25. Harold Holzer, ed., *The Lincoln-Douglas Debates* (New York: HarperCollins, 1993), 174.

26. Zall, *Abe Lincoln Laughing,* 5.

27. Paul M. Angle, ed., *Created Equal?* (Chicago: Univ. of Chicago Press, 1958), 299.

28. Ibid., 335.

29. Page numbers in brackets refer to Holzer, *Lincoln-Douglas Debates.*

30. Lincoln paraphrased a sketch, "Official Report on Central Route," by "John Phoenix"—Captain George Horatio Derby—from the best-selling *Phoenixiana* (New York: D. Appleton, 1853), 19–20, in which the go-it-ometer operator got drunk on lager beer.

31. Lincoln alluded to a popular story about a wife restraining a crowd from interfering in a fight between her spouse and a bear, "Let them fight; for it is the first fight I ever saw, that I did not care which whipped" (*The Humorist's Own Book* [Philadelphia, 1834], 159–60).

32. Lincoln, *Writings and Speeches,* 2:6–7.

33. Ibid., 2:18.

34. "A Hard Case," *Complete Works* (New York: Carleton, 1879), 100.

35. Lincoln, *Writings and Speeches,* 2:127.

36. *Hartford Evening Press,* 6 Mar. 1860; Lincoln, *Collected Works,* 4:13.

37. Bracketed page references are to Lincoln, *Collected Works,* vol. 4.

38. Lincoln, *Writings and Speeches,* 2:272.

39. Ibid., 379–80.

40. William Wirt, *Life of Patrick Henry* (Philadelphia: Desilver, Thomas, 1836), 388–89.

41. Lincoln, *Writings and Speeches,* 2:383–84.

42. Ibid., 457, 460–61.

43. Hay, *Inside Lincoln's White House,* 76.

44. Lincoln, *Writings and Speeches,* 2:530–31.

45. Dudley T. Cornish, *The Sable Arm* (New York: Longmans, Green, 1956), 217.

46. U.S. War Dept., *The War of the Rebellion: A Compilation of the Official Records of the Union and Confederate Armies,* 128 vols. (Washington, DC: Government Printing Office, 1880–1901), ser. 3, vol. 5, 897.

47. Lincoln, *Writings and Speeches,* 2:535.

48. Richard Walsh and William L. Fox, *Maryland* (Baltimore: Maryland Historical Society, 1974), 341, 376.

49. Lincoln, *Writings and Speeches,* 589–90.

50. *New York Herald,* 10 June 1864; Lincoln, *Writings and Speeches,* 2:598–99.

Writings of Others before April 1865

1. J. W. F. White, "Judiciary of Allegheny County," *Pennsylvania Magazine of History and Biography* 7 (1883): 181–82.

2. David C. Means, ed., *Lincoln Papers,* 2 vols. (Garden City, NY: Doubleday, 1948), 1:169.

3. Mitgang, *Abraham Lincoln,* 138.

4. Fred W. Brinkerhoff, "The Kansas Tour of Lincoln the Candidate," *Kansas Historical Quarterly* 13 (1945): 303–6.

5. *Harper's Weekly* 4 (28 Apr. 1860): 259.

6. Roy P. Basler, ed., "J. Q. Howard's Notes on Lincoln," *Abraham Lincoln Quarterly* 4 (1947): 395.

7. *The Salmon P. Chase Papers,* ed. John Niven, 5 vols. (Kent, OH: Kent State University Press, 1993–98), 1:425.

8. *Harper's New Monthly Magazine* 22 (Mar. 1861): 566.

9. Orville James Victor, *Incidents and Anecdotes of the War* (New York: Torrey, [1862]), 79.

10. Hay, *Inside Lincoln's White House,* 19.

11. Rodney O. Davis and Douglas Wilson, *Herndon's Informants* (Urbana: Univ. of Illinois Press, 1998), 85.

12. Mitgang, *Abraham Lincoln,* 274.

13. "Memorandum of General McDowell," in Henry J. Raymond, *Life and Public Services of Abraham Lincoln* (New York: Derby and Miller, 1865), 773.

14. George Templeton Strong, *The Diary of George Templeton Strong: Young Man in New York, 1835–1849,* ed. Allan Nevins and Milton Halsey Thomas (New York: Macmillan, 1952), 3:204–5.

15. Sam Splicem, *Joke Upon Joke* (New Haven, CT: Maltby, Goldsmith, 1818), 95–96; *Addresses Delivered at the Lincoln Dinners in 1887–1909* (New York: Republican Club of the City of New York, 1909), 30–31.

16. Robert S. Harper, *Lincoln and the Press* (New York: McGraw-Hill, 1951), 336.

17. Edward Dicey, *Six Months in the Federal States,* 2 vols. (London: Macmillan, 1863), 1:223, 224; page references in brackets are to this edition.

18. Madeleine Vinton Dahlgren, *Memoir of John A. Dahlgren* (Boston: Osgood, 1882), 370.

19. *Southern Punch,* 24 Oct. 1863, 2 Jan. 1864.

20. "War Gazette," *New York Herald,* 12 Aug. 1862.

21. John Lyle King diary, 8 Jan. 1863, vol. 9, MBV 753, Indiana State Historical Society. Thanks to my friend Michael Vorenberg, who tracked the transmission of this joke for me through King's diary.

22. *Frank Leslie's Illustrated Newspaper* 16 (19 Sept. 1863): 407.

23. Hay, *Inside Lincoln's White House,* 306n79. Succeeding page references in brackets are to this edition.

24. Huntington Library MS, HP 119, 22 Nov. 1863.

25. John M. Schofield, *Forty-six Years in the Army* (New York: Century, 1897), 110.

26. Mark A. Neely Jr., "'Unbeknownst' to Lincoln," *Civil War History* 44 (1998): 214.

27. Paraphrased in *Chicago Tribune*, 30 Oct. 1863.

28. *Magazine of History*, extra number 125 (1926): 34.

29. *Chicago Tribune*, 19 Dec. 1863.

30. Andrew Adderup, *Lincolniana; or Humours of Uncle Abe* (New York: J. F. Feeks, 1864), 88; Zall, *Abe Lincoln Laughing*, 42–43.

31. Samuel L. M. Barlow papers, letter books, 8:8, transcribed by Michael Vorenberg, Huntington Library.

32. George Boutwell in Allen Thorndike Rice, *Reminiscences of Abraham Lincoln by Distinguished Men of His Time* (New York: North American Publishing, 1886), 111; Frank B. Carpenter, *Six Months at the White House* (New York: Hurd and Houghton, 1866), 155; Benjamin Rush Cowen, *Abraham Lincoln: An Appreciation* (Cincinnati: R. Clarke, 1909), 36; Ward Hill Lamon, *Recollections of Abraham Lincoln,* ed. Dorothy Lamon Teillard (Chicago: McClurg, 1895), 194–95; and Huntington Library MS, 151179, 2:132.

33. Fehrenbacher and Fehrenbacher, *Recollected Words,* 482.

34. Daniel Aaron, ed., *The Hales and the 'Great Rebellion'* (Northampton, MA: Smith College, 1966), 44–45.

35. Zall, *Abe Lincoln Laughing,* 33–39.

36. James M. Ashley, *Reminiscences of the Great Rebellion* (Toledo: privately published, 1890), 39; Zall, *Abe Lincoln Laughing,* 6.

37. Benjamin F. Butler, *Butler's Book* (Boston: Thayer, 1892), 304.

38. Noah Brooks, "Personal Reminiscences of Lincoln," *Scribner's Monthly Magazine* 5 (Feb.–Mar. 1878): 564.

39. Rice, *Reminiscences of Abraham Lincoln,* xxvi; Francis Browne, *The Everyday Life of Abraham Lincoln* (New York: N. D. Thompson, 1887), 574; *Harper's New Monthly Magazine* 31 (1865): 136.

40. T. A. Haultain, ed., *Life and Opinions* (London: Laurie, 1913), 290; Goldwin Smith, "President Lincoln," *Macmillan's* 11 (Feb. 1865): 301.

41. Hay, *Inside Lincoln's White House,* 197–98.

42. Ibid., 217.

43. Zall, *Abe Lincoln Laughing,* 32.

44. Hay, *Inside Lincoln's White House,* 217.

45. Zall, *Abe Lincoln Laughing,* 63; Fehrenbacher and Fehrenbacher, *Recollected Words,* 327.

46. *Chicago Tribune,* 25 Dec. 1864.

47. Fehrenbacher and Fehrenbacher, *Recollected Words,* 17.

Stories Told after April 1865 by Those Who Knew Lincoln Well

1. Fehrenbacher and Fehrenbacher, *Recollected Words,* 79.

2. Zall, *Abe Lincoln Laughing,* 48–49. A transcript by Ward Lamon adds, "and I have no head to spare" (Huntington MS, LN2418A, p. 460).

3. Journal entry, 31 May 1865, *Recollections of Alexander H. Stephens,* ed. M. L. Avary (New York: Doubleday, Page, 1910), 137.

4. Zall, *Abe Lincoln Laughing,* 49.

5. Carpenter, *Six Months at the White House,* 131; Byron Johnson, *Abraham Lincoln and Boston Corbett* (Waltham, MA, 1914), 17; Mort Lewis, "Were It Not for This Occasional Vent," *Lincoln Herald* 60 (1958): 89.

6. Raymond, *Abraham Lincoln,* 748.

7. Joseph G. Baldwin, *Flush Times of Alabama and Mississippi* (New York: D. Appleton and Co.: 1853), 24.

8. Douglas L. Wilson and Rodney O. Davis, eds., *Herndon's Informants* (Urbana: Univ. of Illinois Press, 1998), xiv.

9. Fehrenbacher and Fehrenbacher, *Recollected Words,* 249.

10. Representative replies given below derive from the transcript of Herndon's raw notes made in 1866 by John G. Springer and edited by me for *Abe Lincoln Laughing* (1982), cited by page numbers in brackets. Wilson and Davis, *Herndon's Informants,* 737–78, supplies further biographical information about the informants.

11. Fehrenbacher and Fehrenbacher, *Recollected Words,* 150; Wilson and Davis, *Herndon's Informants,* 17n.

12. Wilson and Davis, *Herndon's Informants,* 171; Huntington Library MS, LN 2408, 1:400.

13. Benjamin P. Thomas, *Lincoln's New Salem* (Springfield: Abraham Lincoln Association, 1934), 14, 64.

14. Huntington Library MS, LN 2408, 1:540–43; Wilson and Davis, *Herndon's Informants,* 90–91.

15. *Harper's New Monthly Magazine* 31 (July 1865): 225.

16. Huntington Library MS, LN 2408, 1:127–28; the transcription by Elizabeth Crawford is from 1:186–89 and is also in Wilson and Davis, *Herndon's Informants,* 127, 152.

17. Sir Thomas Urquhart and Peter Le Motteux, trans., *Rabelais Gargantua and Pantagruel* (London: David Nutt, 1900), 233–34.

18. Exhibited in the Philadelphia Library Company's exhibit, October 2000, and reproduced in Robert F. Engs and Randall M. Miller, *The Birth of the*

Grand Old Party (Philadelphia: Univ. of Pennsylvania Press, 2000), 73. My thanks to Mark L. Johnson for calling this to my attention.

19. Huntington Library MS, LN 2408.2.122; Carpenter, *Six Months at the White House,* 284; *Harper's Monthly Magazine* 115 (1907): 524.

20. Huntington Library MS, LN 2408, 2:339; Wilson and Davis, *Herndon's Informants,* 473.

21. Huntington Library MS, LN 2408, 1:473; Wilson and Davis, *Herndon's Informants,* 472.

22. Douglas L. Wilson, *Honor's Voice* (New York: Alfred A. Knopf, 1998), 205–6.

23. Huntington Library MS, LN 2408, 2:214–15; Wilson and Davis, *Herndon's Informants,* 472.

24. Wilson, *Honor's Voice,* 69.

25. Champ Clark, *My Quarter-Century of American Politics,* 2 vols. (New York: Harpers, 1920) 2:198.

26. W. O. Stoddard Jr., ed., *Memoirs of William O. Stoddard* (New York: Exposition Press, 1955), 75; *Wit and Wisdom* (London: J. Smith, 1826), 89–90; *Harper's New Monthly Magazine* 5 (July 1852): 271; *Harper's New Monthly Magazine* 17 (Sept. 1858): 565.

27. William N. Baringer, "On Enemy Soil," *Abraham Lincoln Quarterly* 7 (1952): 18.

28. Isaac N. Phillips, *Abraham Lincoln by Some Men Who Knew Him,* ed. Paul M. Angle (Chicago: American House, 1969), 51–52; Andrew D. White, *Autobiography* (New York: Century, 1907), 2:127.

29. Roy J. Honeywell, *Chaplains of the United States Army* (Washington: Dept. of the Army, 1958), 104–5, 109.

30. Henry Montgomery, *Life of Major-General William Henry Harrison,* 2d ed. (New York: Miller, Orton, and Mulligan, 1857), 456.

31. Wilson and Davis, *Herndon's Informants,* 573.

32. Page references in brackets for anecdotes from *Scribner's Monthly Magazine* are to Zall, *Abe Lincoln Laughing.*

33. R. H. Newell, *Orpheus C. Kerr Papers,* 1st ser. (New York: Carleton, 1866), 285.

34. Paul M. Zall, ed., *Nest of Ninnies* (Lincoln: Univ. of Nebraska Press, 1970), 173–74; Frank Moore, *Anecdotes, Poetry and Incidents of the War* (New York, 1866), 48.

35. I am grateful to Michael Burlingame for transcribing this entry from Townsend's scrapbook at the Library of Congress, 8 Apr. 1993.

36. Egbert Viele, "A Trip with Lincoln, Chase, and Stanton," *Scribner's Monthly* 16 (Oct. 1878): 814.

37. Ibid., 818; Fehrenbacher and Fehrenbacher, *Recollected Words,* 453.

38. Isaac N. Arnold, *Abraham Lincoln: A Paper Read before the Royal Historical Society* (Chicago: Fergis, 1881), 190.

39. Zall, *Abe Lincoln Laughing,* 83, 84 ; Ivan Doig, "The Genial White House Host and Raconteur," *Illinois State Historical Journal* 62 (1969): 311.

40. Zall, *Abe Lincoln Laughing,* 85; Harriet A. Weed, ed., *Autobiography of Thurlow Weed* (Boston: Houghton Mifflin, 1883), 607, 612.

41. Zall, *Abe Lincoln Laughing,* 77; Joshua Fry Speed, *Reminiscences of Abraham Lincoln* (Louisville: J. P. Morton, 1884), 30; *Spirit of the Times* 3 (1857): 319.

42. Thomas James, trans., *Aesop's Fables* (London: John Murray, 1848), 31–32.

43. Zall, *Abe Lincoln Laughing,* 77–78; Speed, *Reminiscences,* 31–32.

44. David Dixon Porter, *Incidents and Anecdotes of the Civil War* (New York: Appleton, 1885), 15–16, 64–65, 294–95.

45. Gideon Welles, *Diary,* ed. Howard K. Beale, 3 vols. (New York: Norton, 1960), 1:333; Fehrenbacher and Fehrenbacher, *Recollected Words,* 181.

46. Lincoln, *Collected Works,* 5:419n.

47. Iona Opie and Peter Opie, *Classic Fairy Tales* (New York: Oxford Univ. Press, 1974), 214.

48. Artemis Ward, *The Complete Works* (New York: Carleton, 1879), 100.

49. Huntington Library MS, LN2418, Ward Hill Lamon, "Administration of President Lincoln," 457.

50. George B. McClellan, *McClellan's Own Story* (New York: Webster, 1887), 162; Zall, *Abe Lincoln Laughing,* 97.

51. Zall, *Abe Lincoln Laughing,* 99.

52. Ibid., 102.

53. Ibid., 100–101.

54. Ibid., 101–2.

55. William H. Herndon and Jesse K. Weik, *Herndon's Lincoln: The True Story of a Great Life,* 3 vols. (Chicago: Belford-Clarke, 1889), 1:317.

56. Zall, *Abe Lincoln Laughing,* 104.

57. 30 June 1888, Huntington Library MS, HM 2029, pp. 21, 22–24, 26, 27–28.

58. Zall, *Abe Lincoln Laughing,* 27–28.

59. Bishop [Henry B.] Whipple. "My Life among the Indians," *North American Review* 150 (Apr. 1890): 438.

60. Undated clipping from *New York Mail and Express,* Judd Stewart scrapbook, Huntington Library MS, 151179, 2:4–5.

61. Henry C. Whitney, *Life on the Circuit with Lincoln* (Boston: Estes and Lauriat, 1892), 179–80, 181.

62. *Independent*, 4 Apr. 1895, 219; Zall, *Abe Lincoln Laughing,* 108–9.

63. Rice, *Reminiscences of Abraham Lincoln,* 393.

64. Teillard, *Recollections of Abraham Lincoln,* 83, 139–40; Zall, *Abe Lincoln Laughing,* 110, 111, 144.

65. Judd Stewart Scrapbook, Huntington Library, accession 151179, 2:31; D. H. Bates, *Lincoln in the Telegraph Office* (New York: Century, 1907), 206–7; Zall, *Abe Lincoln Laughing,* 112, 113.

66. John Hay, "Life in the White House in the Time of Lincoln," *Addresses of John Hay* (New York: Century, 1907), 324–25.

67. Horace Porter, *Campaigning with Grant* (New York: Century, 1897), 221–22.

68. Helen Nicolay, *Personal Traits of Abraham Lincoln* (New York: Century, 1912), 21–22; Zall, *Abe Lincoln Laughing,* 144–45.

Stories Told by Others after April 1865

1. Albert D. Richardson, *The Secret Service, the Field, the Dungeon, and the Escape* (Hartford: American Publishing Co., 1865), 319. Fehrenbacher and Fehrenbacher, *Recollected Words,* 379.

2. George Augustus Sala, *My Diary in America in the Midst of War,* 2 vols. (London: Tinsley, 1865), 2:139, 147–48.

3. Moore, *Anecdotes, Poetry, and Incidents of the War,* 28, 489.

4. Teillard, *Recollections of Abraham Lincoln,* 16.

5. Benjamin Ogle Tayloe, *In Memoriam* (Washington, 1872), 144.

6. Louis Philippe Albert d'Orléans, *History of the Civil War in America,* 4 vols. (Philadelphia: Coates, 1876–78), 1:470–71.

7. Aaron D. Young to Ward Lamon, 26 May–16 June 1886, Huntington Library MS, LN 1399.

8. Browne, *Every-day Life of Abraham Lincoln,* 329.

9. *New York Tribune,* 23 Jan. 1887; clipping in Judd Stewart scrapbook, Huntington Library MS, accession 151179, 2:47.

10. Undated article, *Washington Post,* Judd Stewart scrapbook, Huntington Library MS, 151179, 2:126, about Palmer, who would have been called "Senator" from March 1891 until March 1897.

11. *Detroit Free Press,* 9 Jan. 1898, Judd Stewart scrapbook, Huntington Library MS, 151179, 2:29–30.

12. George B. Wright, "Personal Recollections," *Ohio Archaeological and Historical Quarterly* 8 (1899): 119–20.

13. T. G. Onstot, *Pioneers of Menard and Mason Counties* (Forest City, IL: T. G. Onstot, 1902), 96. Analogues usually have the president replying with some

variant of "Whose shoes do you think I polish?" Zall, *Abe Lincoln Laughing,* 139–40.

14. James Grant Wilson, *Washington, Lincoln, and Grant* (New York: Society of the Order of the Founders and Patriots, 1903), 14. An analogue told by Horatio C. King at the Lincoln Fellowship Dinner, 11 Feb. 1911, has General Oliver Howard, a religious man, in similar circumstances cautioning his driver about swearing, and the driver replying, "If I get religion who in hell is going to drive these mules!" (Huntington Library MS, 2037, p. 33).

15. John McGovern, "Washington and Lincoln," *National Magazine* 23 (Feb. 1906): 524.

16. Henry L. Williams, *Lincoln Story-Book* (New York: Dillingham, 1907), 120, 196.

17. Ellis Paxson Oberholtzer, *Jay Cooke, Financier of the Civil War,* 2 vols. (Philadelphia: G. W. Jacobs, 1907), 1:156.

18. Cornelius Cole, *Memoirs* (New York: McLaughlin, 1908), 173.

19. James Grant Wilson, "Recollections of Lincoln," *Putnam's Monthly and the Reader* 5 (Feb.–Mar. 1909): 673.

20. David Homer Bates, "Lincoln As He Was," *Leslie's Weekly* 8 (4 Feb. 1909): 106.

21. Isaac N. Phillips, ed., *Abraham Lincoln by Some Men Who Knew Him* (Bloomington, IL: Pantagraph, 1910), 99–100, 102–3.

22. Huntington Library MS, HM 2037.

23. William J. Seaver, "Some Impressions of Abraham Lincoln in 1856," *Magazine of History* 14 (Dec. 1911): 244.

24. Thomas Lowry, *Personal Reminiscences of Abraham Lincoln* (Minneapolis, 1910); Zall, *Abe Lincoln Laughing,* 140–42.

25. Stanley Schell, "Lincoln Celebrations," *Werner's Readings and Recitations,* no. 46 (1910), 144–45.

26. Lincoln Fellowship Dinner, 11 Feb. 1911; stenographic transcript by Edmund J. Murphy, Huntington Library, HM 2037.

27. Hay, *Inside Lincoln's White House,* 77.

28. Anthony Gross, *Lincoln's Own Stories* (New York: Harpers, 1912), 84.

29. Ibid., 96; Zall, *Abe Lincoln Laughing,* 146.

30. Lillie de Hegerman-Lindencrone, *In the Courts of Memory* (New York: Harpers, 1912), 65.

31. Champ Clark, *My Quarter Century in Politics,* 2 vols. (New York: Harpers, 1920), 185.

32. Robert W. McBride, *Personal Recollections of Abraham Lincoln* (Indianapolis: Bobbs-Merrill, 1926), 54–55.

33. Carpenter, *Six Months at the White House,* 65.

34. Supplied by Don Fehrenbacher prepublication in Fehrenbacher and Fehrenbacher, *Recollected Words,* 436.

35. Merrill D. Peterson, *Lincoln in American Memory* (New York: Oxford Univ. Press, 1994), 261.

36. Paxton Hibben, *Henry Ward Beecher, an American Portrait* (New York: Doran, 1927), 197.

37. John J. Duff, *A. Lincoln, Prairie Lawyer* (New York: Rinehart, 1960), 339.

38. Paul M. Zall, ed., *Blue and Gray Laughing* (Redondo Beach, CA: Rank and File Publications, 1996), 71.

39. Richard Wolkomer, "Political Insult Ain't What It Used to Be," *Smithsonian* 11 (June 1980): 176; Zall, *Abe Lincoln Laughing,* 161.

40. For the dancing anecdote, see Walter B. Stevens, *A Reporter's Lincoln* (St. Louis: Missouri Historical Society, 1916), 77.

SELECTED BIBLIOGRAPHY

Aaron, Daniel. *The Hales and the Great Rebellion, Letters: 1861–65.* Northampton, MA: Smith College, 1966.

Adderup, Andrew. *Lincolniana, or Humours of Uncle Abe.* New York: J. F. Feeks, 1864.

Addresses Delivered at the Lincoln Dinners in 1887–1909. New York: Republican Club of the City of New York, 1909.

The American Jest Book. Philadelphia: Hogan & Thompson, 1833.

Angle, Paul M. *"Here I Have Lived."* New Brunswick: Rutgers Univ. Press, 1950.

Arnold, Isaac N. *Abraham Lincoln: A Paper Read before the Royal Historical Society.* Chicago: Fergus, 1881.

Baldwin, Joseph G. *Flush Times of Alabama and Mississippi.* New York: D. Appleton and Co.: 1853.

Barrett, Joseph H. *Abraham Lincoln and His Presidency.* 2 vols. Cincinnati: Robert Clarke, 1904.

Bates, David Homer. "Lincoln As He Was Day by Day." *Leslie's Weekly* 108 (4 Feb. 1909): 106.

———. *Lincoln in the Telegraph Office.* New York: Century, 1907.

———. *Address. Proceedings of the Second and Third Annual Meetings.* New York: Lincoln Fellowship, 1910.

Berry, Mildred. "Abraham Lincoln: His Development in the Skills of the Platform." In *History and Criticism of American Platform Address,* ed. W. N. Brigance. New York: Russell and Russell, 1960.

Book of Anecdotes and Joker's Knapsack. Philadelphia: John E. Porter, 1871.

Brooks, Noah. "Personal Reminiscences of Lincoln." *Scribner's Monthly* 15 (1878): 4–5, 561–69, 673–81, 884–86.

Brown, Nathan. "Diary." *Northwest Ohio* 22 (Spring 1950): 61–62.

Browne, Francis F. *The Every-day Life of Abraham Lincoln.* New York: N. D. Thompson, 1887.

Burton, William E. *Cyclopedia of Wit and Humor.* 2 vols. New York: Appleton, 1858.

Carpenter, Frank B. "Anecdotes and Reminiscences." In *The Life and Public Services of Abraham Lincoln,* ed. Henry J. Raymond. New York: Derby and Miller, 1865.

———. *Six Months at the White House.* New York: Hurd and Houghton, 1866.

Chase, Salmon P. *The Salmon P. Chase Papers.* Ed. John Niven. 5 vols. Kent, OH: Kent State University Press, 1993–98.

Cole, Cornelius. *Memoirs.* New York: McLoughlin, 1908.

Congressional Globe 23d–42d Congress. Washington D.C.: Globe, 1834–73.

Conwell, Russell H. *Why Lincoln Laughed.* New York: Harper & Brothers, 1922.

Cowen, Benjamin Rush. *Abraham Lincoln: An Appreciation.* Cincinnati: R. Clarke, 1909.

Dawes, Henry L. "Recollections of Stanton under Lincoln." *Atlantic Monthly* 73 (Feb. 1894): 162–69.

Dicey, Edward. "Washington during the War." *Macmillan's Magazine* 6 (May 1862): 16–29.

Doig, Ivan. "The Genial White House Host and Raconteur." *Journal of the Illinois State Historical Society* 62 (1969): 307–11.

Donald, David Herbert. *"We Are Lincoln Men": Abraham Lincoln and His Friends.* New York: Simon and Schuster, 2003.

Duff, John J. *A. Lincoln, Prairie Lawyer.* New York: Rinehart, 1960.

Fehrenbacher, Don, and Virginia Fehrenbacher. *Recollected Words of Abraham Lincoln.* Stanford: Stanford Univ. Press, 1996.

Foster, Augustus John. *Jeffersonian America.* Ed. Richard Beale Davis. San Marino: Huntington Library, 1954.

Funny Stories, or the American Jester. Worcester, MA: Worcester Book Store, 1795.

Gobright, Lawrence A. *Recollection of Men and Things at Washington during a Third of a Century.* Philadelphia: Claxton, Remsen & Heffelfinger, 1869.

Grant, Ulysses S. *Personal Memoirs.* 2 vols. New York: C. L. Webster, 1885.

Grimsley, Elizabeth Todd. "Six Months in the White House." *Journal of the Illinois State Historical Society* 19 (1926–27): 43–73.

Gross, Anthony. *Lincoln's Own Stories.* New York: Harpers, 1912.

Harper, Robert S. *Lincoln and the Press.* New York: McGraw-Hill, 1951.

Hay, John. *Addresses of John Hay.* New York: Century, 1907.

———. *At Lincoln's Side: John Hay's Civil War Correspondence and Selected Writings.* Ed. Michael Burlingame. Carbondale: Southern Illinois Univ. Press, 2000.

———. *Inside Lincoln's White House: Complete Civil War Diary.* Ed. Michael Burlingame and J. R. T. Ettlinger. Carbondale: Southern Illinois Univ. Press, 1997.

———. "Life in the White House in the Time of Lincoln." *Century Magazine* 41 (Nov. 1890): 33–37.

———. *Lincoln's Journalist.* Ed. Michael Burlingame. Carbondale: Southern Illinois Univ. Press, 1998.

Hegermann-Lindencrone, Lillie de. *In the Courts of Memory.* New York: Harpers, 1912.

Herndon, William H. *Herndon's Life of Lincoln.* Ed. Paul M. Angle. New York: Boni, 1936.

Herndon, William H., and Jesse K. Weik. *Herndon's Lincoln.* 3 vols. Chicago: Belford-Clarke Co., 1889.

———. *Abraham Lincoln: The True Story of a Great Life.* 2 vols. New York: Appleton, 1913.

Hertz, Emanuel. *Lincoln Talks.* New York: Viking, 1939.

Hill, Frederick Trevor. *Lincoln the Lawyer.* New York: Century, 1906.

History of Sangamon County. Chicago: Interstate Publishing, 1881.

Holland, Josiah G. *Life of Abraham Lincoln.* Springfield, MA: Gurdon Bill, 1866.

Holzer, Harold. "Avoid Saying 'Foolish Things.'" In *We Cannot Escape History,* ed. James M. McPherson. Urbana: Univ. of Illinois Press, 1995.

———. *The Lincoln-Douglas Debates.* New York: HarperCollins, 1993.

Howard, James Quay. "Notes on Lincoln." Ed. Roy Basler. *Abraham Lincoln Quarterly* 4 (1946–47): 386–400.

Howard, Joseph, Jr. "Reminiscences of Stephen A. Douglas." *Atlantic Monthly* 8 (Aug. 1861): 205–13.

King, Horatio C. "Address at Lincoln Fellowship Dinner, 11 February 1911." Transcript by Edmund J. Murphy, Huntington Library MS, HM 2037. The Huntington Library, San Marino, CA.

Kyle, Otto R. "Mr. Lincoln Steps Out: The Anti-Nebraska Editors' Convention." *Abraham Lincoln Quarterly* 5 (1948–49): 25–37.

Lamon, Ward Hill. "Administration of Lincoln." Typescript, Huntington Library MS, LN 2418A. The Huntington Library, San Marino, CA.

———. *Recollections of Abraham Lincoln.* Ed. Dorothy Lamon Teillard. Chicago: A. C. McClurg, 1895.

Lincoln, Abraham. *Collected Works.* Ed. Roy P. Basler, Marion D. Pratt, and Lloyd A. Dunlap. 8 vols. New Brunswick: Rutgers Univ. Press, 1953–55 and supplements.

———. *Lincoln Papers*. Ed. David C. Mearns. 2 vols. Garden City: Doubleday, 1948.

———. *Writings and Speeches*. 2 vols. Ed. Don E. Fehrenbacher. New York: Library of America, 1989.

Locke, David Ross. *Nasby Papers*. Indianapolis: C. O. Perrine, 1864.

Lowry, Thomas. *Personal Reminiscences of Abraham Lincoln*. Minneapolis: privately printed, 1910.

McBride, Robert W. *Personal Recollections of Abraham Lincoln*. Indianapolis: Bobbs-Merrill, 1926.

McClellan, George B. *McClellan's Own Story*. New York: Webster, 1887.

McClure, Alexander K. *"Abe" Lincoln's Yarns and Stories*. Philadelphia: Winston, 1901.

McGovern, John. "Washington and Lincoln." *National Magazine* 23 (Feb. 1906): 518–25.

Miller, Joe. *The Family Joe Miller*. London: William S. Orr, 1848.

———. *Joe Miller's Jests*. London: T. Read, 1745.

Mitgang, Herbert. *Abraham Lincoln, a Press Portrait*. New York: Fordham Univ. Press, 2000.

———. *Lincoln as They Saw Him*. New York: Collier, 1962.

Moore, Frank. *Anecdotes, Poetry and Incidents of the War*. New York, 1866.

———. *Rebellion Record*. 11 vols. New York: Van Nostrand, 1861–68.

Newell, R. H. *Orpheus C. Kerr Papers*. 1st series. New York: Carleton, 1866.

Nicolay, Helen. *Personal Traits of Abraham Lincoln*. New York: Century, 1912.

Oberholtzer, Ellis Parsons. *Jay Cooke, Financier of the Civil War*. 2 vols. Philadelphia: Jacobs, 1907.

Old Abe's Joker. New York, T. R. Dawley, 1863.

Oldroyd, Osborne H. *Lincoln Memorial: Album Immortelles*. New York: Carleton, 1882.

Onstot, Thompson Gaines. *Pioneers of Menard and Mason Counties*. Forest City, IL: T. G. Onstot, 1902.

Paris, Comte de. *History of the Civil War in America*. 4 vols. Philadelphia: Coates, 1876–78.

Peterson, Merrill D. *Lincoln in American Memory*. New York: Oxford Univ. Press, 1994.

Phillips, Isaac N., ed. *Abraham Lincoln by Some Men Who Knew Him*. Bloomington, IL: Pantagraph Printing, 1910.

Porter, David Dixon. *Incidents and Anecdotes of the Civil War*. New York: Appleton, 1885.

Porter, Horace. *Campaigning with Grant*. New York: Century, 1897.

Pratt, Harry E. "Illinois As I Knew It." *Papers in Illinois History* (1937): 109–87.

———. *Illinois as Lincoln Knew It*. Springfield: Illinois State Historical Society, 1938.

Raymond, Henry J. *Life and Public Services of Abraham Lincoln*. New York: Derby and Miller, 1865.

Rice, Allen Thorndike. *Reminiscences of Abraham Lincoln by Distinguished Men of His Time*. New York: North American Publishing, 1886.

Sala, George Augustus. *My Diary in America in the Midst of War*. 2 vols. London: Tinsley, 1865.

Sandburg, Carl. *Abraham Lincoln: The Prairie Years*. 2 vols. New York: Harcourt-Brace, 1926.

———. *Abraham Lincoln: The War Years*. 3 vols. New York: Harcourt-Brace, 1939.

Schofield, John M. *Forty-six Years in the Army*. New York: Century, 1897.

Schouler, James. "Abraham Lincoln at Tremont Temple." *Massachusetts Historical Society Proceedings* 42 (1909): 70–83.

Seaver, William J. "Some Impressions of Lincoln in 1856." *Magazine of History* 14 (Dec. 1911): 242–47.

Segal, Charles M., ed. *Conversations with Lincoln*. New York: Putnams, 1961.

Shakespeare's Jests of 1867. London: R. Sharpe, n.d.

Shaw, George W. *Personal Reminiscences of Lincoln*. Moline, IL: Carlson, 1924.

Smith, Henry Martyn. "Western Reminiscences." *Proceedings of the Worcester Society of Antiquity* (1879): 32–45.

Speed, Joshua Fry. *Reminiscences of Abraham Lincoln and Notes of a Visit to California*. Louisville: J. P. Morton, 1884.

Splicem, Sam. *Joke Upon Joke*. New Haven, CT: Maltby, Goldsmith, 1818.

Stanton, Henry B. *Random Recollections*. 2d ed. New York: Macgowan and Slipper, 1886.

Stephens, Alexander H. *Recollections of Alexander H. Stephens*. Ed. M. L. Avary. New York: Doubleday, Page, 1910.

Stevens, Walter B. *A Reporter's Lincoln*. St. Louis: Missouri Historical Society, 1916.

Strong, George Templeton. *The Diary of George Templeton Strong: Young Man in New York, 1835–1849*. 4 vols. Ed. Allan Nevins and Milton Halsey Thomas. New York: Macmillan, 1952.

Tarbell, Ida. *Life of Abraham Lincoln*. 4 vols. New York: Lincoln Historical Society, 1900.

Tayloe, Benjamin Ogle. *In Memoriam.* Washington, DC, 1872.

U.S. War Dept. *The War of the Rebellion: A Compilation of the Official Records of the Union and Confederate Armies.* 128 vols. Washington, DC: Government Printing Office, 1880–1901.

Victor, Orville James. *Incidents and Anecdotes of the War.* New York: Torrey, 1865.

Viele, Egbert. "A Trip with Lincoln, Chase, and Stanton." *Scribner's Monthly* 16 (Oct. 1878): 813–22.

Ward, Artemus. *The Complete Works.* New York: Carleton, 1879.

Ward, William H., ed. *Abraham Lincoln: Tributes from His Associates.* New York: Crowell, 1895.

Weed, Thurlow. *Autobiography.* Ed. Harriet A. Weed. Boston: Houghton-Mifflin, 1883.

Welles, Gideon. *Diary.* Ed. Howard K. Beale. 3 vols. New York: Norton, 1960.

Whitney, Henry Clay. *Life on the Circuit with Lincoln.* Boston: Estes and Lauriat, 1892.

Williams, Henry L. *Lincoln Story Book.* New York: Dillingham, 1907.

Wilson, Douglas L. *Honor's Voice.* New York: Alfred A. Knopf, 1998.

Wilson, Douglas L., and Rodney Davis. *Herndon's Informants.* Urbana: Univ. of Illinois Press, 1998.

Wilson, James Grant. "Recollections of Lincoln." *Putnam's Monthly and the Reader* 5 (Feb.–Mar. 1909): 515–29, 670–75.

Wilson, William B. "Abraham Lincoln." Huntington Library MS HM 2029. The Huntington Library, San Marino, CA.

Wit and Wisdom. London: J. Smith, 1829.

Wright, George B. "Honorable David Tod." *Ohio Archaeological and Historical Society Publication* 8 (Oct. 1899): 101–25.

Zall, Paul M. *Abe Lincoln Laughing.* Berkeley: Univ. of California Press, 1982. Reprint, Knoxville: Univ. of Tennessee Press, 1997.

———. *Blue and Gray Laughing.* Redondo Beach, CA: Rank and File Publications, 1996.

———. "Abe Lincoln Laughing." In *The Historian's Lincoln,* ed. Gabor Boritt. Urbana: Univ. of Illinois Press, 1988.

———. *Lincoln on Lincoln.* Lexington: Univ. Press of Kentucky, 1999.

INDEX OF ENTRIES BY SECTION

1. Lincoln's Writings and Speeches

1838
Ms. Owens rejects blockhead suitor, 1

1839
New York Dems have running itch, 2

1841
Squirrel hunter fires at louse, 3

1842
Paddy defers to Judgment Day, 3–4

1848
AL can't keep in order, 4
McFingal's gun kicks over owner, 4
Patrick's new boots need stretching, 4
Congressman is hooked by hooker, 5
Cass's war record compares to AL's, 5
New York Dems divide like hogs, 6
Pants fit man or boy, 7

1849
AL deprecates his signature, 7

1852
AL mocks Franklin Pierce's life, 7–8
Widow lost faith as britchen broke, 8

1854
Cattle loosed in meadow, 9
Two plus two does not equal four, 10

1856
Tom wants to reborrow wheel-
barrow, 10
Victim offers robber his note, *10*
Woman tells ugly man to stay home,
10
AL says Buchanan is in cat's paw, 11

1858
Chestnut horse is not horse chestnut, 12
AL covets flattery like gingerbread, 12
Douglas relies on go-it-ometer, 12–13
Widow says set body for more eels, 13
Douglas plan is homeopathic soup, 13
Wife favors neither husband nor bear,
13

1859
Adam and Eve invented sewing circle,
14
Drunks fight into other's coat, 14

1860
Killing robber would make a mur-
derer, 14–15
Horse is fatted up to its knees, 15

1861
Slow horse misses convention, 15
Train pulls out before AL ends, 15–16
AL says quiet man is hard to find, 16
AL exchanges looks with ladies only,
16
Lincolns are long and short of it, 16

1862
Lady's sons are rare workers, 16
AL asks McClellan what tired horses,
17
P. Henry's speculator cried "Beef," 17

1863
Juror would rather hang the jury, 17
AL puns on voyeur as peeper, 18
AL avows avoiding dog beats a bite, 18
AL says erudition not for officers, 18

1864
Sheep and wolf disagree on liberty, 19
Farmer won't swap horses mid-
stream, 19

2. Writings of Others before April 1865

1849
Old Virginian strops razor, 21
Old woman's fish grows as handled, 21

1859
AL too hurt to laugh or too proud to cry, 21–22

1860
AL puns lake should be Minneboohoo, 22
First man pulls blanket off third, 22

1861
Camp follower taps cider barrel, 23
AL asks if Maryland can bury 75,000, 23
AL plays dumb on senator's district, 23
Ugly man told to shoot uglier man, 23–24
Sow has more pigs than teats, 24

1862
AL would borrow McClellan's idle army, 24
Parson won't cross till comes to river, 25
Barber shaves cheek, cuts his finger, 25
Folks with no vices have few virtues, 26
Innkeeper keeps no dying guests, 26
Slave owner complainants conflict, 26
Farmer kills one skunk, lets rest go, 26
George III tells mad Wolfe to bite others, 26–27
AL says one wife at a time is enough, 27
Irish plan new jail from one in use, 27

1863
AL puns on act of Congress and wife, 28
Villager Billy Bray defies draft, 28
AL says death penalty scares convict, 28
AL condemns deserters as they run, 28
Lawyer advises going to Tennessee, 29
AL sees army as shovels of fleas, 29
If Christ had come, would not again, 29
Chin-fly makes the horse go, 29–30
Preacher's powder ain't worth damn, 30
AL's says rebels drink worse whiskey, 30
Child's squall means not dead yet, 30

Steam doctor mangles medical terms, 30
AL claims Lord likes common people, 30–31
AL heard no ill of general for year, 31
Irishman asks for drop "unbeknownst," 31
AL as a boy plowed around stumps, 31
Lady says Lord will think AL joking, 31–32
AL can now give variola to all, 32
AL says shot would not have hurt girl, 32–33

1864
Farmer says powder's been shot, 33
Wife told to sleep with Supervisor, 33
Irishman hears frogs as only noise, 34
Joe will "go troo de wood," 34
AL cannot wash black white, 34–35
AL thinks visitor came to preach, 35
AL places Capitol within mile of hell, 35–36
AL prices lieutenant at sixteen horses, 36
AL makes generals cheaper than horses, 36
AL boasts twelve hundred thousand men, 36
Legless soldier gets tract on dancing, 36
Drunken Swett fends off feeding frenzy, 37
Bill asks help letting bear go, 37
Pompey fooled by three-pigeon riddle, 38
Worthless dog must be good for coons, 38
Damndest scoundrel is also damndest fool, 38
AL allows wrigglers to wriggle, 39
Exploded dog is not much account as a dog, 39–40

1865
AL wants migrants striking out not in, 40
AL would be hard put to outpull his team, 40
AL interfering would enlarge kitten hole, 40

3. Stories Told after April 1865 by Those Who Knew Lincoln Well

1865

AL remembers Charles I lost his head, 41–42

Farmer would rather let hogs root, 42

Webster in school shows dirtier hand, 42

AL has little pull with administration, 43

Judge insists on which hand blew nose, 43

Boy losing apple asks to stop boat, 44

Landlord cannot stop for fire elsewhere, 44

AL asks where Niagara's water came from, 45

AL humbly proclaims his politics in 1832, 45

Preacher slaps at lizard, kicks off pants, 45–46

Liar is believed only if corroborated, 46

AL asks if swift mare drew short breaths, 46

AL tickles bedded girl's feet and above, 47

AL says a wife's only flaw is her spouse, 47

AL admits foe's insanity as hereditary, 47

AL pens saga of cross-bedding bride-grooms, 47–48

AL pens ballad about a same-sex marriage, 48

1866

Brave fighter appeals to be held back, 49

Millerite births for the neighborhood, 49

Ethan Allen cures Brits' constipation, 49–50

Old man scoffs at so many swift horses, 50

AL cares not for hat but showman's eggs, 50

Toper takes drunk's arm for pump handle, 50–51

AL says lost case will be seen in hell, 51

Sow's log opens to outside not inside, 51–52

Boy wishes his coon would run away, 52

AL disdains lightning rod for guilt, 53

AL fools pest with fake love letter, 53

AL exposes Taylor's aristocratic finery, 53–54

AL composes poem on symbiotic sex, 54

AL riddles on why woman is like barrel, 54

Winfield Scott says details spoil bust, 54–55

Boy deflates Daniel Webster as "great," 55

Traveler asks more light, less noise, 55–56

Farmer will test suspect spinach on Jake, 56

AL gives up reading, just signs papers, 56

AL gets knife from less ugly man, 57

Lady's poodle is used to swab windows, 57

Westerner mutilates law terms, 58

Cooper puts boy inside to hold up top, 58

Boy fears Shadrack, Meshach, Abednego, 58

Wife benefits from abusing her husband, 59

AL warns scorched will sit on blisters, 59

Boy lacks mud to make a minister, 59–60

Tyler offered best train if dead, 60

AL feels like Patagonian eating oysters, 60–61

1867

AL jests with biblical allusion, 61

1869

AL repeats same allusion, 61–62

AL says the state sends all little men, 62

1878

Welles studies Noah's ark for navy, 62

Picket says send hard-tack not generals, 62–63

Soldier bets mug cannot be smashed again, 63

Tad's turkey is too young to vote, 63

Old juror decries stealing hens vs. sheep, 64

Old lady says fan can kiss her elder ass, 64

Boy says horse has what's good for him, 64–65

AL confesses one vice, he can't say no, 65

1881

Pat wants to vote for rebellion side, 65–66

1882

Bill cons clerk of cider and cornbread, 66

AL hints law for private to hit captain, 67

1883

Old man discounts fifteen years in Maryland, 67

Sausage maker receives two cats, 67

1884

Chickens wait to be tied for travel, 68

Lion in love is disarmed, dismissed, 68

1885

Gambler and preacher switch jobs, 69

Husband can't tell rabbits from skunk, 69

Office seeker settles for trousers, 69

1886

Monkey's tail bears him down, 70

Blacksmith settles for fizzle, 70–71

Son asks whose wife to take, 71

AL puns on "stirring" argument, 71

Saying tail is leg won't make it a leg, 71

Army uses noses to avoid mud, 71–72

AL leads his men through a gate, 72

Westerner takes nothing but money, 72

AL says eight office seekers sicker, 72–73

AL queries why God sends via Chicago, 73

Condemned says no fun till he gets there, 73

General would have died years ago, 73

AL okays interracial unions with proviso, 74

AL never gets between axe and skillet, 74

Virginians would queue at North Pole, 74

Rebel yells cure colonel's boils, 74

Patricide pleads mercy as orphan, 75

1887

Man says building is a foot broad, 75

Generals made now, quartermasters next, 76

Ladies' man entered flesh but once, 76

Preacher is too lazy to stop writing, 76

Irishman says name is on the letter, 77

Golliher swaps his for AL's hat, 77

Polecat looks, acts, smells, and is, 77

Hog stealer freed, sold hogs to jury, 78

Man of audacity carves turkey, 78

Boy wants to get she cat with kitten, 79

Landlord always kills whole critter, 79

1888

Child is black from hips down and up, 80

AL says he's president not fire chief, 80

AL compares no news to no luck, 80

AL puns on fast workers on fast day, 80

AL avoids words with "by" as swearing, 80–81

1890

Indian agent needs ten honest watchers, 81

1892

AL cons comrades on creek crossing, 81

Blower fits most words in fewest ideas, 82

1895

Farmer hullos while people are passing, 82

Daughter has only two bastard babies, 82–83

Boy howls to show how hard he works, 83

Farmer only wants what joins his land, 83

1896

Man has no feet, pants sweep snow, 83–84

AL puns on suspending hanging, 84

Merchant's powder would survive hell, 84

1912

Pioneer mother is nearly out of Bibles, 85

4. Stories Told by Others after April 1865

1865

Indian pony eats only cottonwood, 87
AL tells lady her family did enough, 87–88

1866

AL had no ancestor older than father, 88
AL wants respite from "Mister," 88
AL reassures, nobility no impediment, 88
Man if has to die wants that disease, 88
Farmer told to stick to business, 88–89
Newsboy says AL's phiz will improve, 89
AL contributes naught to end in view, 90
Irish captain not on speaking terms, 90

1867

Terrier triumphs since always mad, 90
Judge excepts women and children, 91

1869

Toper says mouth holds just a pint, 91

1872

Preacher-type "don't care a damn," 92

1875

Preacher ignored, adds mare lost, 92

1876

Dogs bark, fence falls, they run off, 92–93

1886

AL at front fears no rebel sharpshooter, 93
AL will go home when given a pass, 93
AL asks if troops want only shirts, 93

1887

Old man says self-made AL did bad job, 93–94
Judge suspects other side may be worse, 94

1897

Dwarf after giant makes digger speak, 94–95

1898

AL recommends evaluating rat hole, 95

1899

Governor Tod points to only one "d" in God, 95
Inventor's auger bores itself out, 95–96

1901

Lincoln boys each want two of three nuts, 96
Washington's swearing makes Corwin happy, 96
Visitor asks prisoner how to get out, 96–97
Preacher and toper are hopeless minority, 97

1902

AL asks whose shoes gentlemen do shine, 97

1903

Patient was Columbus by another mother, 97
AL says driver swears like Episcopalian, 97–98

1906

AL could not hold conversation with gents, 98

1907

Boy sets hen on forty-three eggs to spread herself, 98–99
Lady says laird's puir head his only one, 99
AL quips beard darker since jaws used more, 99
Child recovery seen when "down to raisins," 99
AL could have told her hat would not fit lady, 100
AL turns out for folks, avoids collisions, 100
Girl answers, "Knee deep and a sixpence," 100

1908

Parson told all will be saved, hopes not, 101

1909

"Perfect woman" was husband's first wife, 101
AL tells of hen-walker and hen-persuader, 101–2

AL assures that bugs will leave good suit, 102

John Moore loses steers or finds cart, 102–3

AL talks about fooling people at times, 103

Balloonist mistaken for Jesus, 103–4

1910

Girl's sad dancing made up for by turns, 104

Boy says any fool can see he's playing, 104

AL says legs should reach the ground, 104–5

Boy says dad is under load of hay, 105

Boy says he'll get the hang of spelling, 105

Squire rejects his practice as unlawful, 105

1911

Man tarred, feathered would rather walk, 106

1912

Witness takes in "swarin' for a livin'," 106

AL responds to spiritualist's manuscript, 106

AL knows two songs as stand up or not, 107

1920

AL knows several who'd take his chair, 107

1922

Fish scales weigh baby at forty-seven pounds, 107

Brit puts clothes abed, self over chair, 107–8

Ward raised corn, neighbor hogs ate it, 108

Ward's crows brought back stolen corn, 108

1924

AL says Dems use argumentum ad womanum, 108

1926

AL says God knew why to curl pig's tail, 108–9

1926–27

AL claims Todd in-laws get worst of it, 109

AL is candidate to come or stay away, 109

1939

Chief says why sun never sets on empire, 109

Man claims there's man in automaton, 110

Farmer wishes he'd never seen squirrel, 110–11

Boy knows all about river always here, 111

Simpkins can fiddle shirt off Jones, 111–12

Ma Partington's broom challenges sea, 112

1980

Hooker misplaces headquarters in saddle, 112

1994

AL wants to dance in worst way and does, 113

AL hears new hats gone two hours ago, 113

2003

AL puns T. R. Strong, coffee stronger, 113

SUBJECT INDEX

A

Absent-minded Englishman, 107–8
Adam, Eve and, 14
Aesop, quoted, xiii–xiv, 34, 68
Agent, Indian, 81
Allen, Ethan picture, xviii, 49–50
Ancestry, AL's, 88; noble, 88
Argument, 71; ad womanum, 108
Aristocracy, 53–54
Army: AL borrows, 24; as fleas, 29;
    avoids mud, 72; wants shirts, 93
Audacity, man of, 78
Auger, bores both ways, 96
Automaton, man inside, 110
Axe, and skillet, 74

B

Baby, weighed, 107
Barber, cuts finger, 25
Barrel: boy in, 58; woman like, 54, 113
Bastards, two, 82–83
Bear: in hole, 11; fighting husband, 13
Beard, gray, 99
Beecher, Henry Ward, on AL, 110
Bible: boy fears trio, 58; gathering of
    eagles, 61; nearly out, 85; perfect
    woman in, 101
Black Hawk war, xvi, 5
Blacks: AL turns out for, 100; as equal,
    12; greeting balloonist, 103–4;
    marriage, 108; washing, 34
Blacksmith, and fizzle, 70–71
Blanket, shared, 22
Blister, heat, 59
Boat, stopping, 44
Boil, cured, 74
Book, critiqued, 106
Bostonians, censorious, xviii
Boy: and apple, 44; and Bible, 58; and
    cat, 79; and coon, 52; and horse,
    65; at school, 105; cooped up, 58;

counting legs, 71; cursing, 104;
    dad in hay, 105; dirty hands, 42;
    deflates D. Webster, 55; farmer's,
    xiv; howling, 83; out of mud, 60
Bray, Billy, drafted, 28
Bridegroom, in wrong bed, xviii;
    47–48
Buchanan, James, as cat's paw, 11
Butler, Benjamin F., and pass for AL,
    93

C

Calhoun, John, as adversary, 8–9
Candidate: for supervisor, 33; AL too
    much of a, 109
Capitol, distance to White House,
    35–36
Cass, Lewis, war record, xvi, 5
Cervantes, Miguel, and Don Quixote,
    7
Chair, White House, 107
Charles I, head lost, 41–42
Chase, Salmon P., 23, 108; and presi-
    dency, 29, 34, 37, 39
Chicago: and God, 73; newsboy, 89
Chicken: pioneer, xiv, 68; stealer, 64
Child: and raisins, 99; black from hips,
    80; squalling, xiii, 30
Chin-fly, 29–30
Christ, second coming, 29. See also
    God; Jesus
Cider: and con man, 66; siphoned, 23
Common people: as audience, xiv; as
    God-favored, 30–31
Congress: Act of, and Mary Lincoln,
    28; AL in, 105; and White House,
    34; vs. Army, 111–12
Congressman, and whore, 4–5
Con man: and cider barrel 23; and
    cider clerk, 66; and fellow
    travelers, 81

Convict: and death penalty, 28; and honor, 106; as orphan, 75; in suspense, 84; no fun without, 73
Coon, and boy, 52; and dog, 38
Cooper, and boy, 58
Cooper Union, AL at, xviii, 14, 15, 22, 107–8
Creek, crossing:, 19, 25, 81. *See also* River
Crockett, Davy: as model, xvi
Crow, and scarecrow, xiii, 108
Cutts, James, alias Count Peeper, 18

D

Dance: AL's wish to, 113; girl's turning, 104; tract on, for legless soldier, 36
Daughter: farmer's, xiv; with two bastards, 82–83
Davis, Jefferson: escape of, 52; lacks marksmen, 93; praying man, xx, 31–32
Death: favored, 88; penalty, a fright, 28
Debates: in Congress, 4, 6; in state legislature, xv–xviii, 3; with S. A. Douglas, xvii, 7–8, 11–13
Democrats: and Republicans, 14; as gang of hogs, 6; old, and self-made AL, 93–94
Deserters, condemned, 28
Digger, and dwarf, 94–95
Disease: favored, 88; vaccination, xvii; variola, 32
Doctor, examination, 99. *See also* Steam Doctor
Dog: always mad, 90; at fence, 92–93; as swab, 57; killing as cure, 18
Don Quixote, and chivalry, 7–8
Donkey, drafted, 28
Douglas, Stephen A.: and debates, xvii, 7–8, 11–13; and go-it-ometer, 12–13; and popular sovereignty, 13; lack of logic, 7; loss of confidence, 8; mocked, 12; short legs of, 104–5
Drunk: coat exchange, 14; hopeless minority, 97; lost cart, 102–3; mistaken pump handle, 50–51; mouth capacity, 91
Dwarf, pursuit of giant, 94–95

E

Eels, and drowned husband, xi, 13
Emancipation Proclamation, xix, 34–35

England: and America, 92–93; and Trent Affair, 97
English: absentminded, 107–8; as dandies, 97; constipation cure, 49–50; in dark, xi, 109
Episcopalian, W. H. Seward as, 98
Eve, and Adam, 14

F

Family: enough service of, 87–88; of Todds, 109
Farmer: and adjacent land, 83; and daughter, xiv; and passerby, 82; and rooting hogs, 42; and pig's tail, 108–9; and skunk, 26; and squirrel, 110–11; war plan of, 88–89
Fast Day, worker on, 80
Father: advice of, 71; AL as, 63, 96, 98; under hay, 105
Feet, sweep snow, 83–84
Fiddler, and preacher, 111–12
Fighter, needing restraint, 49
Fire: at other end of house, 44; blisters from, 59
Fish, old woman's, 21
Fisherman: knowledge of river, 111; scales, 107
Fizzle, blacksmith's, 70–71
Fleas, Army as, 29
Franklin, Benjamin, and oysters, xiii
Fremont, John C., vote against, 108
Free Soilers, and slavery, 6–7
Fun, needing convict, 73

G

Gambler, and preacher, 69
Generals: and whiskey, xiii; feud with Congress, 111–12; headquartered in saddle, xviii–xix; mad, 27; made now, 76; unheard of, 30; unwanted, 62–63; vanity of, 73. *See also* Officer
George III, and mad general, 27
Giant, pursuit of, 94–95
Gingerbread, as favorite, 12
Girl: AL tickles, 47; and dancing, 104; interrogating wounded soldier, xi, 32–33; Scots and eggs, 100
God: and AL joking, xx, 31–32; and Chicago, 73; and common people, 30–31; distrusts English, xi, 109; one "d" enough for, 95

Go-it-ometer, in John Phoenix sketch, 12
Grant, Ulysses S.: drinking, xiii; as presidential candidate, 88
Greens, suspect, tested, 56
Gun: for ugly man, 24; kicking, 4; louse in sight, 3

H

"Hail Columbia," AL song, 107
Hand: D. Webster's dirty, 42; nose-blowing, 43
Hanging, suspended, 84
Harrison, William Henry, and Lewis Cass, 5
Hat: chalked, 10; new, 113; swapped, 77; value of, 50; woman on, 100
Hawthorne, Nathaniel, description of AL, xii
Hay: dad under, 105; farmer's daughter in, xiv
Headquarters, in saddle, xviii–xix, 112
Hell: and lost case, 51; distance from Capitol, 35–36; powder in, 84
Hello, and passerby, 82
Hen: and inventions, 101–2; spreading self, 98–99; stealing, vs. sheep, 64. See also Chicken
Henry, Patrick, quoted, 17
Hog: and open-ended log, 52; fat for neighbors, 108; fewer teats, xviii, 24; New York Democrats as, 6; stealer free, 78; tail, 108
Hood, Thomas: cartoon by, xix; sketch, 99
Hooker, Joe, headquarters of, 112
Horse: and chin fly, 29–30; and horse chestnut, 12; breathing, 46; fatigued, 17; fat to knees, 15; Indian pony, 87; mounting or mounted, xiv; too slow, 15–16; excess of fast, 50, with whatever is good, 64–65
Hunter, mistaking louse, xv–xvi, 3
Husband: first wife, 101; mistaking skunks, 69; wife's flaw, 47; wrestling bear, 13

I

Indian: and British Empire in dark, 109; and pony, 87
Innkeeper: and dying guests, 26; and fire, 44; killing whole critter, 79

Insanity, inherited, 47
Inventions, for hens, 101–2
Irish: ballad, "Cork Leg," xiv, 2; boots sized, 4; drink unbeknownst, 31; legs run away, 2–3; name on letter, 77; new jail and old, 27; new voter, 65

J

Jesus: no second coming, 9; old slave's greeting, 103–4. See also God
Judge: advice to young lawyer, 94–95; fines for women and children, 91; licensing, 105; rigid rules of evidence, 43
Juror: and hen-stealing, 64; would hang jury, 17
Jury, and purloined pigs, 78

K

King: Charles I headless, 42; George III, and bites, 27
Kiss, and antique ass, 64

L

Ladies man, and flesh, 76
Lady: deprived of view, xv, 16; no smut before, xviii; on AL joking, xx, 31–32. See also Woman
Lamon, Ward H., and end in view, 90
Lawyer: advising Tennessee water, 29; amateur, mangles terms, 58; and false witness, 106; assets of, 95; bad company, xviii; lost case in Hell, 51; young, seeking advice, 94
Lee, Robert E., escape of, 52
Leg: length of, 104–5; runaway, 2–3
Letter, mock love, 53
Liar: lying for living, 106; needing corroboration, 46
Liberty, for sheep and wolf, 19
Lightning: less noise, 55–56; rod for guilt, 53
Lincoln, Abraham: and Congress, 28, 35–36,; and dialect, 11, 92; and smutty stories, xviii, 47, 48, 54; and Todds, 109; as candidate, 109; as captain drilling, 72; as common man, xii; as Congressman, 4–9; as dancer, 113; as jokester, xii, xviii–xix, 53, 113; as lawyer, xiv; as legislator, xv, 2–3;

Lincoln, Abraham (cont.)
  as president, xvii; exhausted, 56;
    gravitas, xii, xvi; in Boston, xvii, xviii;
    influence, 43; one vice, 65
Lincoln, Mary Todd: and Act of Con-
    gress, 28; and AL's dancing, 113;
    marriage, 109; meeting in outhouse,
    xviii; short of it, 23; visiting card,
    xvii–xviii, 28
Lincoln, Robert, at reception, 98
Lincoln, Tad, and turkey, 63
Lion: Democrats as, xiii; in love, 68
Loafer, advice to, 89
Locofocos, unmasked, 77

M

McClellan, George B.: and fatigued
    horses, 17; as lost visitor, 96–97; mili-
    tary inaction, 24
Marriage: henpeck benefit, 59; miscege-
    nation, 108. See also Wife; Husband
Maryland: liberty defined in, 19; resi-
    dence discounted, 67; room for
    corpses, 23
Medicine: benefit of variola, 32; termi-
    nology mangled, 30
Mexican-American War, at Monterey, 90
Millerite, prolific wife, 49
Minnehaha, pun on, 22
Missouri Compromise, discussion on, 26
Money, sole acceptable gift, 72
Monkey, anchored by tail, 70
Mother: nearly out of Bibles, 85; of
    pseudo-Columbus, 97; welcoming a
    child's cry, xiii, 30
Mud: Army barrier, 72; out of, for a
    preacher, 59–60

N

New Orleans, balloonist at, 103–4
New York, Democrats of, 6
News, no, 80
Newsboy, and AL's hair, 89
Niagara Falls, source of, 45
Noise: frogs as, 33–34; storm as, 55–56

O

Office Seeker: eaten by bugs, 102; others
    sicker, 72–73; will work for pants, 69

Officer: and gate, 72; and Caesar's hair,
    18; boil cure, 74; cone of silence, 90;
    law for privates, 66–67
Orphan, as patricide, 75
Owen, Robert Dale, seeking critique,
    106
Owens, Mary, courtship of, 1–2

P

Pants: and Lamon, 90; and preacher,
    45–46; office seeker request, 69;
    peddler's, xvi, 7; snow sweeper,
    83–84
Pardons, as oyster shells, 60–61
Partington, Mother, and tide, 112
Patagonians, and oyster shells, 60–61
People, and fooling, 103
Phoenix, John, and go-it-ometer, 12
Pierce, Franklin, biography of, 7–8
Pigeon, in homeopathic soup, xiv, 13; in
    riddle, 37–38
Pig. See Hog.
Plowing, and stump, 31
Poems, by AL: on bridegroom, 48; on
    same-sex marriage, 48; on whoring,
    54
Politics, of AL, 44
Polygamy, AL on, 27
Popular Sovereignty: Stephen A.
    Douglas on, 13
Powder: of preacher, 30; Hell proof, 84;
    recycled, 33
Preacher: and gambler, 69; and perfect
    wife, 101; announcer of lost mare, 92;
    cursing, 92; lazy, 76; not mud enough
    for, 59–60; outfiddled, 111–12; slaps
    at lizard, 45–46; sermon competitive,
    100–101; sleeper awakes as hopeless
    minority, 97
Presidency: and little influence, 43;
    Democrats reject Republican, 14–15;
    honor of, 106; not fire chief, 80
Prisoner, and lost visitor, 96–97

R

Rabelais, Francois, as source, 49
Rebel: Irishman wants to vote as, 65–66;
    whiskey worse, 30; yell cure for boil, 74
Republicans, difference from Demo-
    crats, 14; and slavery, 108

River: boy expert on, 111; preacher won't cross, 25; farmer won't swap in middle of, 19
Robber: offered note, 10; would be murderer, 14–15

S

Sandburg, Carl, on AL wannabe, 111
Sausage, and cats, 67
Scots: laird's head, 99; girl gauges brook and eggs, 100
Scott, Winfield, and bust, 55
Senator, and complaint, 23
Seward, William H.: as Episcopalian, 98; puns with AL, 113
Shakespeare: Falstaff allusion, 1; Hamlet: allusion, 18; quoted, 89
Sheep, and liberty, 19
Shields, James: alleged mad, 26–27; Pierce supporter, 7–8
Signature: without reading, 56; insignificant, 7
Skunk: acts, looks, etc., 77; and rabbits, 69; only one killed, 26
Slave: and balloonist, 103–4; dissatisfied owners, 26; wit combat, 37–38
Slavery: and Free Soilers, 6–7; and Republicans, 108; and territories, 9
Soldier: and gate, 72; bet on mug, 63; tract on dancing, 36; greeting AL, 93; inaction, 108–9; warning AL, 93; wants: hardtack, 62–63; shirts 93; wound, 32–33
Son: choice of wife, 71
Song: AL's on same-sex marriage, 48; knows only two, 107
Springfield, IL, and second coming, 29
Squirrel: and farmer's oak, 110–11; and louse, xv–xvi, 3
Stanton, Edwin M.; and influence, 43; and White House guard, 108–9
Steam Doctor, mangling medical terms, 30
Steer, lost, 102–3
Suitor, AL as, 1–2; lion as, xiii–xiv, 68
Supervisor, and wife, 33

T

Tail: and leg, 71; and pig, 108; of monkey, 70

Tod, David, and one "d," 95
Todd Family, marriage into, 109
Train: interrupting story, 15–16; for Tyler, 60
Traveler: chicken as, 68; in storm, 55–56
Turkey, carving, 78; Tad's, 63
Tyler, John, and train, 60

U

Ugly Man: and knife, 57; threat, 23–24; told to stay home, xv, 10

V

Vanity, of dead general, 73
Variola, contagious, 32
Vice: no, no virtue, 25–26; of AL, 65; of G. Washington, 96
Virginian: at North Pole, 74; and razor strop, 21
Vote: Irish rebel 65–66; turkey ineligible, 63
Voyeur, as Count Peeper, 18

W

Ward, Artemus (Charles F. Browne): "High Handed Outrage," xix; quoted, 108
Washington, George: as cure, 49–50; inmate as, 97–98; profanity, 96
Webster, Daniel: deflated, 55; hand of, 42
Wedding, same sex, 48
Welles, Gideon, 69
Wheel-barrow, borrowed, 10
Whiskey: and Grant, xiii; of rebels, 30; unbeknownst, 31
White House: guard, 98–99, 108–9; chair, 107; Eliza Grimsley at, 109; shoe shine at, 97
Whore: congressman and, 5; verse on, 54
Widow, sets husband again, xi, 13
Wife: benefit, 59; black, 74; choice of, 71; neutral, 13; one enough, 27; only flaw, 47; overbearing, 49; perfect, 101; supervisor's, 33
Witness: professional, 106; unreliable, 46
Wolf, and liberty, 19

Woman: AL not a, xv, 65; and ancient ass, 64; and fish, 21; inquisitive, 32–33; like barrel, 54, 113; perfect, 101; sitting on hat, 100. *See also* Lady

Words: and fewest ideas, 82; of pseudo-lawyer, 58; of steam doctor, 30; profanity, 80–81, 96

Workers: fast, 80; sons, 16

Wound: amputated legs, 36; queried, 32–33

Writing, too lazy to stop, 76

Y

Yankee, peddler, 7

Yell, rebel, as cure, 74

ABE LINCOLN'S LEGACY OF LAUGHTER was designed and typeset on a Macintosh computer system using InDesign software. The body text is set in 8.75/11.75 Century Old Style and display type is set in Britannic Compressed Medium. This book was designed and typeset by Stephanie Thompson and manufactured by Thomson-Shore, Inc.